First published as a collection in 2020

© Maria Alfieri, 2020

A CIP catalogue record for this book is available from the British Library.

Hardback ISBN: 978-1-9163416-0-9

Paperback ISBN: 978-1-9163416-1-6

eBook ISBN: 978-1-9163416-2-3

Disclaimer

This book is to educate and provide general information. The authors and publisher have taken reasonable precautions in the preparation of this book and believe the facts presented are a true and accurate representation of their own experiences.

The Silent Scream:

An Anthology of Despair, Struggle and Hope

Maria Alfieri

PONTEM

Contents

1   **Introduction**

8   *Honour My Story*

11   **Forgiveness & Letting Go**

13   This. Is. Me: A Journey to Empowerment
18   *Forgiveness is...*
21   Time
25   *Letting Go...*
27   Alcohol & Co-dependency
31   After the Discard
35   Rejection
37   When Hurt People, Hurt People
46   I Am Enough
50   This. Is. My. Truth.

59   **Courage**

61   Courage Doesn't Need to Roar
66   Cancer and PTSD
71   Life is Not a Destination
74   *Denial of Pain*
77   Inside I Am Screaming
82   *Miscarriage*
85   *It twists inside*
86   Coming Full Circle
89   *The Lie You Sold*
91   Drowning on the Inside
97   *Running*
99   A Self-Portrait
104   *Women Together*
105   *Echoes*
105   *Finding Balance*
107   *Who Am I?*

109   **Breaking Free**

110   UnShamed
123   Just Me
125   *Taking Shelter from the Storm*
126   The Dark Art of the Heart
129   Break Away
139   Hungry Ghost
146   *Caught in the Web*
148   *Ugliness is just a State of Mind*
151   *The Underlying Causes of my Eating Disorder*
153   I AM

161 Escaping Demons

162 Addiction
169 *Black Bird*
170 *Achilles Heel*
171 *Safety*
172 *Storm*
173 *Torn*
175 *Back Seat Passenger*
177 Numb
181 *Demons*
182 *Alone in the Dark*
183 *Invisible Wounds*
184 *Darkness*
187 *How it Felt when You Said...*
188 *The Unbroken*
189 Stolen

195 Metamorphosis

197 Transformation
198 Redemption
201 Never Enough
205 The Notebook
206 *When there is Nothing Left of Me*
209 Restoration
215 *Sometimes*
217 Mitigating Mental Chatter
218 Knowing Your Worth
220 *I'm automatically drawn...*
221 *Depression is...*

223 Hope

225 Claire
233 Anxiety and Depression
240 Life Can Change in a Moment
245 The Better Way to Life
251 *Gratitude for Bodies*
252 Moses
256 In The Wake of the Walking Wounded
263 Parenting and Mental Health
267 *Kate and Her Wolves*
269 *Sometimes You Can't See the Wood for the Trees*
271 *Living on the Surface*
273 *Imagine*
275 *Step into the Sunshine*
277 Final message

278 Endnotes / Resources / Photography Credits / Contributors

Introduction

"I believe the three most important words anyone can say are not I love you, but I hear you." Oprah Winfrey

Anyone being consumed by their pain and suffering will understand the need to be heard, the need to have their feelings acknowledged and validated, to know that they are not alone in the swirling chaos of their rage, grief and fears, which we mask behind our smile as we make our way through the world. Yet, paradoxically, it seems the hardest thing to do at times; to give voice to our struggles, our feelings, our fleeting moments of madness for fear of being judged, ashamed and embarrassed by our imperfections. And so, we remain trapped in those silent screams, continually feeding our deepest fears about ourselves; that we are not worthy, berating ourselves and internalising our trauma, becoming disconnected and isolated in our experiences.

But when we cannot find a way of telling our story, our story begins to tell us. We develop symptoms, habits- addictions even, behaviours that we don't understand, the truth of our pain working its way to the surface through any means possible, giving expression to the silent scream inside. Our constricted shame-based sense of who we are keeps us trapped in the cycle of self- sabotaging behaviours, which impact both our physical and emotional wellbeing. Our silence only reinforces that shame, inflating the ego which becomes a repressive agency under which we bury our authentic self. But until we can live more consciously, away from the masks and less through the ego, we will never be free from our destructive patterns, or our negative self- talk, which perpetuate our feelings of unworthiness.

It is through our vulnerability that our liberation from our inauthenticity starts. Through honest conversation we break down that fourth wall, which traps us in the illusion of our shame and isolation. We are never alone in our experiences. We are not broken, merely flawed, imperfect and messy, the same as any other human being on this planet. In sharing our stories we can become active observers of our thoughts and feelings, rather than passive passengers of our unconscious behaviours. We expose the falseness of our mind narrative, our self-realisation equipping us with the awareness needed to heal our wounds and interrogate the artifice of the dominant ideologies presented to us.

This process of exposition starts with the unravelling of our parental and social conditioning; the rules and boundaries passed down to us from culture and religion. The dogma which keeps our spirit bound and gagged. The indoctrination that would keep us enslaved to a system of consumerism where we will always be insufficient as we are. We need to break down those walls and stop identifying with form and start identifying as form*less*; beings of infinite potential. When we deny our spirit and go against our instinctive nature, forcing and contorting ourselves to fit a mould too limited to contain our being, we suffer. Our mental and emotional health decline because our focus is on becoming that thing which we are not. And we punish ourselves for it. Or we comfort ourselves with substances and behaviours which help to mask those feelings of unworthiness for just a while. And why wouldn't we? No one ever taught us that the solution to our suffering lies within; that nothing outside of us is ever going to fix us. Our inadequacy makes for profitable business.

Excavation of the soul takes great courage. It means venturing into unknown territory to rediscover the person you were meant to be. It is a messy, chaotic and uncomfortable journey. It means letting go of patterns and behaviours that no longer serve you, creating space for new track to be laid. You'll have to rewire your brain to go against most, if not all, of the things you were taught your entire life.

Many of us as children were told to 'be quiet' and to not 'answer back'. We were disciplined at home and in school for daring to speak up or speak out. We were trained from a young age to swallow our opinions, our feelings, our struggles, the message being that as children our voices did not matter; a habit that became so ingrained, that by adulthood we continued to shut down, unable to express our thoughts, feelings and opinions. We learned that we were not enough, that we needed to change. We learned to stuff down the feelings that were too uncomfortable to bear and suppress the true essence and whisper of our soul.

We grew into wounded adults, self-medicating with food, alcohol, drugs, shopping, sex, co-dependent relationships and various other forms of addiction to numb the pain of our 'not-enoughness'. We became masters of our own betrayal, keeping up appearances to hide the depth of our suffering inside. And we remained silent, too afraid to be seen as anything less than perfect. Intentionally or not, we were taught to conform and obey the rules. Boys had to 'toughen up' and girls had to be 'ladylike'. We were taught to seek out external markers of our success, our gender dictating what those external markers would be. We inherited from our parents their own emotional childhood baggage and the cultural ideals of the society in which they grew up, nobody knowing any different, or the damage it caused to our spirit. And as parents and carers of children ourselves, we repeat the same mistakes and many more besides.

In this age of technology, where we are more connected than we have ever been, our feelings of isolation and disconnection couldn't be any higher. We are becoming increasingly separated and isolated from the Self with increasing external pressures. Our children are also being raised to be disconnected not only from the truth of who they are, but from their family and their peers, interaction happening all too frequently through screens and speakers, technical devices being used as baby sitters, replacing all real human connection and interaction.

We remain unconscious as parents about the effects of our own behaviour on our children, still battling through our own emotional burdens from our childhood, our children's resistance often triggering our ego and causing the ensuing parent/child conflict. We shout at them to 'hurry up' and become infuriated by their reluctance to live life at our speed, our anxious minds always living in the future and the knowledge that time is short and our to-do list is long. Children are merely living in the present moment; the man-made concept of time has not yet stolen the joy from their lives. They are not deliberately attempting to make us angry and stressed. Those feelings are triggered in us because of *our* resistance to live life instinctively and mindfully in the way that children do. *We* are the ones setting terms and conditions to which our children never agreed. *We* are angered when our terms and conditions are not met, and then add a twist of hypocrisy when we expect our children to listen and move on cue and yet don't model the same.

How many times when they ask us for our time do we say, "I'll be with you in a minute," with that minute turning into two, and then three, and then many more minutes besides? How many of us ever actually get around to *really* listening to our children- getting down on their level, looking them in the face and truly hearing each and every word they say? We may allow them to 'whinge' and 'complain' at us whilst we continue with the chores, or vaguely make out some complaint or other over the sound of keys being pressed on whatever device that currently holds our attention, but do we ever stop, and in that moment give our children the attention that *they* need? We are so consumed by our own conditioning to do, to perform, to achieve, that our own children's demands- *needs*- are left unmet, the thing they wanted to tell us dismissed as insignificant by the very way in which we often respond to them.

In this quick-fix instant world we live in, we don't have the patience or the time for ourselves, let alone our children, and so our children are forced into hiding themselves, just as we were, internalising their struggles because they are led to believe they are a slave to a system of control and domination. And that is a belief they will carry with them through life, just as we carried these beliefs; we conform and 'fit in' or we are outcast, rejected - disconnected- which intensifies our feelings of self-doubt and unworthiness. Is it any wonder therefore, with so much disconnection that self- harm is becoming epidemic amongst children and teenagers?

The Millennium Cohort Study found that 16% of the 11,000 14 year olds surveyed reported they had self-harmed in the last year- that's 100,000 children aged 14 and under based on these figures. 22% of girls and 9% of the boys said they had hurt themselves on purpose in the year prior to the questionnaire, with more than a fifth of 14 year old girls interviewed admitting to self- harming. NHS data released in August 2018 showed the number of admissions to hospital of girls aged 18 and under for self- harm had almost doubled in two decades between 1997 and 2017.[i]

With poor mental health being the number one reason for staff absence,[ii] and overall deaths by suicide increasing by 10.9% in 2018,[iii] we must rethink the very foundations on which we build our lives. We have to stop hiding behind the façade of social media profiles and stop buying into the fake reality of others, which only perpetuates the cycle of inauthentic expression. We need to stop wasting energy concealing our shame, projecting only the parts of us which we deem acceptable, and focus on destroying the system which preys on our insecurities, confirming our beliefs that we are not smart, thin, fit, beautiful and rich enough. We need to stop judging ourselves and others for not fitting a standard created by those driven by the ego and all the false values the ego seeks to attain. We need to change the culture of how we view our mental and emotional wellbeing; how we talk about it, how we view it as signs of weakness and hide it for fear of judgement. Moreover, we need to stop suffering in silence.

Silence not only hurts. It kills. Silence breeds shame. It keeps us trapped in isolation, but as humans we are wired for connection. The labels we attach to ourselves- our diagnoses, our gender, race, religion to name but a few- are divisive; they keep us boxed and categorised and away from what truly connects us all; our *humanity*. It takes a tremendous amount of courage to share your story, to feel vulnerable and exposed, the truth of *exactly* who you are out there for the world to see. Yet through vulnerability comes an incredible amount of power and connection, and this is a huge catalyst for healing, growth and change. Know that, as you read this book, the decision to contribute will not have been taken lightly by the co-authors. Yet each has shared from the heart and bared their soul knowing that if *one* person takes something away from their story, that's one more person on the path to their own healing. As collaborators we have come together to say: me too. *I've suffered. Not in the same way as you. But I understand your despair and struggle and I offer you hope.*

So, let's do it. Let's reconcile ourselves- it starts with us. Let's face our deepest fears that we are not enough, unworthy, invalid and insignificant and let's raise our children to do the same, so that we can grow as a collective in love, understanding and compassion. Let's release our pain and suffering by surrendering our ego defences and false masks, for it is through becoming vulnerable that we will discover our true and essential invulnerability.[iv]

So, I refer you back to the beginning, where I started:

The three most important words anyone can say to you are not I love you, but
I hear you.

Because more than anything in life, we fear being insignificant and un-loveable, not worthy enough of having our pain and hurt acknowledged. But being heard provides us with the acknowledgement we crave as part of a system, develops our self-worth and a sense of equality where all voices matter and no one voice is heard above anyone else. It keeps us connected; it brings understanding and healing. And that is where forces join to create a path of love; love for self and love for each other. So let's come together in our fears by sharing them, facing them and healing them, for fear is the great divider and love conquers all.

If together we feel, together we heal.

Maria Alfieri

Honour My Story

Libraries of love, pain, passion and grief all woven together with spines hard, pages thin and words scribbled down.

To read my story I have to invite you to open me up.

To honour my voice, as you skim over the bits you don't want to see.

You are blessed to be able to turn the page, but for me this is my history.

Honour my story.

Honour my sorrow.

Honour my soul.

You are a beautiful book that I'd be blessed to read, yet know it is yours.

You own your past.

You are the narrator.

And what a gorgeous gift it is to be a teller of stories, of adventure and of hardship.

The next chapter is waiting for you. It is time to start writing.

Kate Morgan

Forgiveness
&
Letting Go

This. Is. Me: A Journey to Empowerment   13

Forgiveness Is...   18

Time   21

Letting Go...   25

Alcohol & Co-dependency   27

After the Discard   31

Rejection   35

When Hurt People, Hurt People   37

I Am Enough   46

This. Is. My. Truth.   50

This. Is. Me.
A Journey to Empowerment

Lost

I was eight years old the first time your penis touched the back of my throat. I remember the gagging sensation as you forced my head down; my small lungs struggling for air as I drowned in your phallus.

I recall the sour taste, the worry that you would wee in my mouth. I remember the panic and not really understanding what was going on.

You disappeared when you'd finished, leaving me confused and frightened on the bed. When you returned, my trousers came down. I lay limp beneath your malevolent touch, my voice and body taken hostage by fear. It was our secret. If I told anyone, I'd be taken away. Social Services always came for girls like me. I swallowed that lie. And it changed me.

My soul fragmented with the shame; your darkness leaked into those cracks. I was stained. Unworthy. Telling someone, anyone, was an impossibility; to speak the truth would be to detonate a bomb of dishonour on my family. Or at least that's what I thought. You taught me that the girl you had sullied was no longer loveable. And so, I rejected her. I wanted nothing to do with *that* disgusting girl.

It started with small things, little ways to punish myself for allowing myself to be enslaved to you in that way. I'd hit myself in anger. *Just tell someone.* But I couldn't. My mouth incapable of forming the words. I began to wonder if this was normal. *Maybe this happens to everyone?* I remember prodding my friends at primary school, trying to find out if this had been happening to them too. Of course, I didn't reveal anything about my own humiliating experience.

By the time I was nine or ten, I concluded that I was very much alone in this experience. To have my body used and touched for another person's pleasure without my consent was not normal. And it was certainly not acceptable.

And yet, I *had* accepted it. By saying nothing. At least, that is the narrative I told myself. As I grew older, the *sex* word started being thrown around the playground. Kids would laugh and take guesses as to what it meant, what it involved. I soon realised that that was what this was. It was *sex*.

I was eleven years old and I had been having forms of sex with you already for three years. I really *was* that girl. A dirty slut- another word that I had heard batted around by other kids. That sense of being un-loveable and unworthy really began to cement itself. With all my might I wanted it to stop. But wrongfully, I thought I had no power over you. I was just a little girl. This was bigger than me. And I was being lost to it. Engulfed by a power, a system bigger than my own.

I wanted to trade the body I was in. To remove the blemish you'd marked me with. It started innocently. I just wanted to lose a few pounds. I began to leave out treats. Skip meals. As the weight dropped off, I found a way to cope with my burden; a physical demonstration of the pain I could not vocalise. That quickly spiralled into starving myself into almost non-existence. My parents and doctors closed ranks. Finally, I was safe from you.

But that wasn't enough. Safety, I mean. I required escape. Escape from the reality of being me. By the time I was thirteen years old, I was hospitalised. I had thrown myself out of moving cars, taken razor blades to my skin and developed a fear of eating. I was on bed rest and calorie count. And when I continually refused to eat and dropped yet more weight, I had a tube put up my nose to keep me alive. But it was a life I no longer wanted; the wounds you scourged inside me festered toxically. I needed to numb the pain of being me.

Found

I became addicted to self -destructive habits, switching one for another, compelled by some death drive that you triggered in me; always trying to escape *that* girl and the body I was in; the woman in me sentenced to silence by the innocent child that you stole. She was not worthy of a happy life, a carefree life. She must continue to suffer. *I* must continue to suffer the consequences of carrying around inside of me that same un-loveable girl that you tainted. I spent my teens and my twenties living life through the fear that I was nothing more than the shameful mess you reduced me to. For many years I believed this lie. *Twenty seven years* to be exact; literally a life sentence. The punishment I served for your sins.

Your sins.

The day I acknowledged this, I recovered the woman in me. A tired, weary and dishevelled one, but a woman nonetheless. And I found the lost child too. Not the un-loveable one, but the loveable, happy girl from before. The girl with hopes and dreams. The girl that was always there- just out of reach.

I shifted my thinking, awakening the true power inside of me, the power I always had over you; this wasn't *my* cross to bear. I hadn't somehow inherited your sins. I could separate myself from the things *you* did to me and so, I assigned the blame to where it belonged; with you.

I no longer had to hate myself, detest my body and carry that shame. That baggage is and always was, yours. And so, I put that cross down and handed it to you. And then I forgave you.

I forgave *you*.

And it set me free.

I found that muted voice - the one which once wilted with shame. It wants to be heard. It *deserves* to be heard. So, I am here, yelling at the top of my lungs:

I AM LOVEABLE.

I AM WORTHY.

It's still difficult to hear at times; that I am loveable. That I am worthy. It is hard to accept that the chaos is okay. *I* am okay. Every day I wrestle that fear and walk towards the light. I have to step out of those old shadows because fear has no place in a life based on love. And love is the only cure, the only way to heal the cracks of my fragmented soul and make me whole again.

The road to self -love is not an easy one. It is unfamiliar and uncomfortable and at times, unnatural to me; my darkness is still easily seduced by the relief of those old addictive, self -destructive habits that help to either punish or reject the unacceptable parts of me. But I can see that now for what it is. And when I find myself rejecting those messy, stained, parts of me- the unlovable child- I decide to embrace them instead. To love them. Self - compassion is necessary to staying true to who we are.

Despite the suffering, I wouldn't change being lost to you. As the saying goes: *sometimes we need to lose what needs to be lost, in order to find what needs to be found.* Losing myself to you meant having to find myself. And not the fear based, ego-driven identity of who I think I should be. But the true me. The authentic me. The me that is not afraid to walk in the path of the truth of who I am. So, it's all here. My mess. My truth. For all to see. Completely and unapologetically.

This. Is. Me.

Maria Alfieri

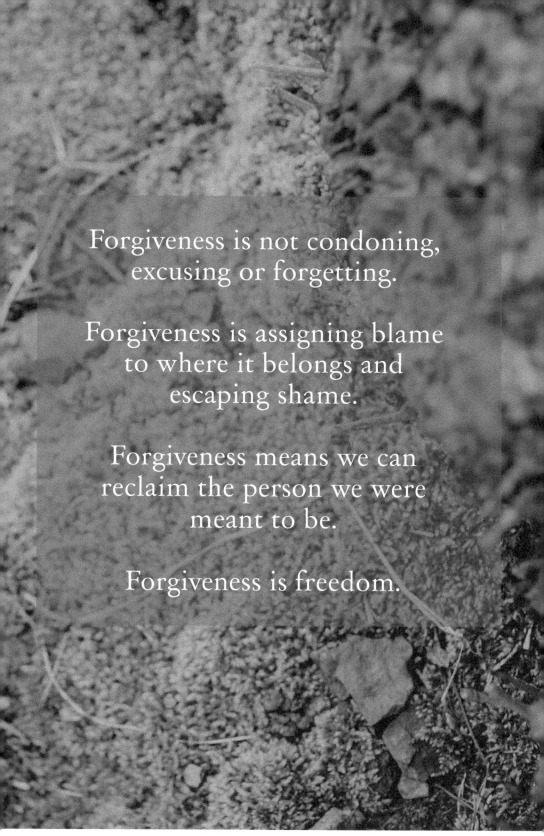

Forgiveness is not condoning,
excusing or forgetting.

Forgiveness is assigning blame
to where it belongs and
escaping shame.

Forgiveness means we can
reclaim the person we were
meant to be.

Forgiveness is freedom.

Time

I have spent many hours pondering how best to write about my experiences. These hours have passed in work and play, rushing about living the life I now live and love. Time has been spent playing with my children, commuting, writing reports and doing the mundane things in life.

It's only now, as I'm chasing time to write this, that I've truly realised how easily and quickly time has actually slipped through my fingers.

It hasn't always been this way.

I remember, as clear as if it were yesterday, although decades have now passed, how every hour, minute and second that ticked by hurt. I felt this in every part of my being...it was unbearable. I had to make it stop.

The dull, all-pervading ache would be ever present in my body; my mind sluggish but hyper alert to every conversation, look and expectation. I was very much a perfectionist back then, and probably am still now to a degree. For a while I managed to use this to cope with how I was feeling. I threw myself into learning and achieving; I had to be the best, then everything would be ok and the pain would go away. It worked. For a while. Or so I thought.

I kept myself so busy and under so much pressure that I didn't notice at first. I thought if I just kept going it would get better. It had to get better because I couldn't carry on feeling this way. But my lack of self-worth was still there buried underneath the perfectionist working herself into exhaustion.

I ate less and did more. I found freedom in dance but soon lacked the energy to keep going. So, I ate even less and worked even more. In my mind I'd failed at dancing, so I had to achieve elsewhere. The pressure mounted and the cracks started to show. Thinking in a straight line became harder and harder, time slowed down and each day felt like an entire lifetime. Nights became a waking nightmare as sleep evaded me and my thoughts threatened to drown me:

You're a failure and always will be.

You're irritating and everyone hates you.

Worthless, ugly, pathetic.

Stupid.

You let everyone down.

One night the negative self-talk became too much. I needed to find a way to stay afloat. In the early hours, all alone, I was desperate. Reaching for my craft scissors, I drew them across my skin. A long thin line of red bloomed and I felt better, freer, calmer. So, I did it again and again.

That night I found my best friend and worst enemy. Self-harm made the hours, minutes and seconds of the day easier to tolerate. It calmed my thoughts and eased my pain. For the first time I had a focal point for my pain; it was no longer silent and trapped inside. I could manage life again if I had my blade at my side.

What I didn't know at the time was that this would become my coping strategy for many years to come. But by hurting myself I wasn't fixing the problem, I was only putting a bizarre sticking plaster around my feelings that would always fall off. When it did I'd pick up the blade and hurt myself again.

Those minutes and hours I was surviving turned into years. The self-harm became more extreme as I became used to the effect on my body. When I wasn't hurting myself, it felt like fire ants were racing through my veins, my mind was boiling and I would end up broken in a million pieces on the floor.

It was no longer worth trying to survive the hours; even the minutes and seconds felt impossible. I tried to take my own life and ended up in hospital. This became a pattern that repeated many times; the best friend I thought would help me through became the enemy that was intent on killing me.

I think it came close, although now on reflection, there are big gaps in my memory. I don't know if I had simply checked out of life for a while, or the pain was too great and my mind has put a barrier up to protect me. But I'm pleased; I don't care to remember that dark time with complete clarity. It would hurt too much.

I can hear you asking, *what changed?* You're here writing about a family and a life you now love. Something must have happened to make living more bearable. It didn't. Well, nothing huge and definitely not fast. I realised that I could die trying to escape my pain, or I could give facing it a try. At that point I had nothing to lose.

So, I made little changes. I started talking properly to people again. I hadn't done that in a very long time; after all, I was worthless and useless, who on earth would want to listen to me? It turned out they did. And there were many people in my life who wanted to help. I just had to find the right ones and trust it.

Some wanted to keep me safe and take care of me...whilst this was appreciated, it felt limiting. I needed people around me that could hold my hope for a better, more fulfilling life, people that could see beyond my scary behaviour and help me realise my potential.

I found a GP who would talk to me about books (a great passion of mine) instead of always focusing on the bad things.

A boyfriend (now partner and father of my children) who would hold me when the fire ants descended, and didn't judge or get angry if I needed to harm.

A university tutor who encouraged me and showed me what I could do.

Friends who never let me down, who I could contact regardless of how long it had been since we last spoke, and wanted to spend time with me.

I allowed myself to try being the person I wanted to be. Most of all, I allowed myself to fail and try again. I learnt that we all hurt and we all fail. It's what we do with these experiences that counts.

Now I try to be the best me I can but recognise that sometimes I get it wrong. I own the mistakes and learn from them. Don't get me wrong, it wasn't easy and there have been many ups and downs, but once I had a taste of what a real life could be, I didn't want to go back to tolerating the seconds, minutes and hours. When the fire ants descend now (and they still do) I have a mantra: *how do I solve this problem?*

I have tools in my box to do this; I can talk it out, sleep on it or do a calming exercise and then address it. I am not powerless to my feelings anymore and consequently I'm not always in pain.

Life now is still a roller coaster, but that's how it is supposed to be, laughing with the kids, battling the trains or speaking at an event. Each second, minute and hour spent make my life worth living.

Suki

Let go of the past and the patterns that no longer serve you...

Alcohol & Co-Dependency

I had a shit time when my parents split up, which happened to coincide with my final year of A-Levels. Things had been going sour between them for some years previously, which meant they'd developed an interest in trying to protect their own individual happiness; there was little room for guiding me through a crucial period of my education. As a result, I chose the wrong A-Levels, not playing to my linguistic strengths and instead I batted my head against science and geology. I had for a long time had the fantasy of spending my life in a shark cage, gawping at and studying great white sharks, hence the scientific choice of subjects. But I was fluent in French and scored top marks in Latin, Greek and German...had I chosen those subjects at A-Level, I might not have been the dismal failure I was when it came to results day. Oh well!

The years that immediately followed were very tough. I was living at home with an abandoned parent, who themselves were clearly having a very tough time of it too. They consistently, over a good couple of years, used the bottle both as a crutch to get through the pain and unhappiness of a failed marriage, and also as relief of the stress of having to play the role of both parents. I slowly and perhaps invariably became co-dependent to the remaining parent. This included having to be incredibly sensitive to their mood when they came home, especially if they'd had a few drinks. I too was recruited in their search for escape, being asked and expected to keep refilling their wine glass from the fridge at home. I had become an 'enabler' of alcoholism, and I had absolutely no idea. Any initial resistance was met with fire, and it was best for the mood of the entire household (my sisters were at home too) to do as I was told.

Couple this with already low self-esteem at being 'left behind' not just by a parent, but my contemporaries as they all went off to university, I was utterly miserable and fell into a deep depression, the first episode of it in my life.

Fast forward fifteen years and I found myself in Dubai, having been headhunted for a senior position in a PR agency. I had never even been to Dubai but I had always wanted to work abroad and jumped at the chance. I don't think I was running away from my life in London, but the opportunity to start afresh and cut some of the mental baggage was irresistible. I didn't look back.

About a year after I arrived in Dubai, I started going out with a girl who I worked with. The early days were a lot of fun. Dubai is a party-town and with a party invariably comes alcohol. Lots of alcohol. The first few times we got drunk together at some of Dubai's notorious brunches, all seemed OK. Well, just about OK. My girlfriend would get that little bit more drunk than everyone else and I became somewhat anxious, but didn't show it as I didn't want to tarnish what I felt was a burgeoning relationship. I put the over-indulgence on her part down to 'over-exuberance' or lack of a proper dinner. What I failed to see was that these were warning signs and my 'easy acceptance' of this was learned behaviour from fifteen years previous, when I had been co-dependent to another important and influential woman in my life: my mother.

Months went by and we fell in love, enjoying weekends away in the smart desert hotels that were just a short drive from the hustle and bustle of the city, but seemed like a different world altogether. One on one, away from the party atmosphere, we drank in moderation and generally had a wonderful time in each other's company.

In the second year however, things started to change. Her drinking stepped up, not in frequency, but in the binge amounts and subsequent levels of drunkenness. I remember all too well that when we were out together at a party or a social bar/club based gathering, I would wait for the moment, the one sip of a cocktail that would tip her over the edge. My lovely girlfriend would become someone else altogether. A stranger. A person with a wild look in her eyes for whom our relationship, our bond and our love, faded into the nothingness of a drunken haze. I would instinctively become her 'guardian', keeping a watchful eye, making sure she didn't snap her tongue at a stranger for looking at her funny, or stumble into a group of people as she tottered drunkenly around in heels. She would say nasty things to me when drunk and on one occasion even bit me. I was no longer myself either. I had reverted back to the subservient, fearful teenager I once was, unable to take hold of the situation for fear of the consequences.

Much to my chagrin, she would never remember anything the following morning, of how I had to practically carry her out of the club with her slumped on my shoulder, past countless judgemental looks and sneers of 'your girl's wasted' and accusations of me 'using ruffies'. I once had to stop a taxi while she fell out and collapsed onto the pavement, almost into the gutter, clearly unable to take care of herself in any way. I felt so frustrated, but was bound by the psychological chains to be 100% co-dependent to her. I felt I had no choice. My own happiness and emotions were pushed aside, as they had been before, but instead of a parent it was my girlfriend - obviously a very different dynamic, but nonetheless, I was co-dependent to a woman once again.

I batted my head against this wall of pain for many more months. In sober moments, I would try to understand from 'where the demons came' and explore the reasons behind her wish to get paralytic. Not only to help her, but also to allow me to try and understand for myself. Sadly, in spite of much effort she never opened the door. Around this time I had taken the step to go and see a psychiatrist for support in my own battle against anxiety and depression. They gave me the strength to listen to my own voice inside my head and slowly but surely, helped me rebuild enough self-esteem to realise that I had to leave the relationship. I still think that had she opened the door to 'let me in', we could have battled our individual demons together, which in turn would have built the foundation for a potential life-long relationship.

I remain philosophical. Everything happens for a reason and while I still think of her, I look back on our relationship as the lesson that taught me to get over the previous lesson around alcohol and co-dependency. I am grateful for both experiences – they have made me who I am. They have proved that I do have self-esteem and that I am in full control of that. It has also taught me that nearly all other things in life are beyond my control and in knowing that, I am free. I have also learned that life is not about things that happen to you but about how things happen for you. It's how you choose to react. These painful occurrences have given me the strength to nurture and own that vital power.

Tom Conway-Gordon

After The Discard

I know now why you picked me. The insecurity, anxiety, co-dependency, fear...

There was no real substance in the monsters I made,

The same can't be said of the 'Jekyll' you played.

You were a monster on the inside,

Using the mask of a good man to hide.

Nothing was real and I'm left broken-hearted,

Healing the wounds you ripped open and started.

What you labelled love was really abuse,

Using the pain of your past as an excuse.

I felt unworthy, but that isn't true;

There won't ever be supply sufficient for you.

Now you are gone and my new life begins,

And I will let NO ONE else pay for your sins.

All of my demons now under control,

But you will go on with that void for a soul.

Emotional abuse is often covert and insidious, and because of the poor way we've come as humans to relate and connect in romantic relationships in general, it can be difficult to recognise too. When does it start to become a toxic or abusive relationship rather than just a 'bad' relationship? People often have difficulty with these labels, as they feel that maybe they are being too 'dramatic' or 'over the top'. There are a plethora of behaviours which under law would be definable as emotional abuse, including criticism, intimidation, excessive financial control, gas lighting...to name but a few.

The important thing to consider when asking yourself if you might be in an abusive relationship is, *how do you feel in yourself within this relationship?* If you feel belittled, like you're walking on eggshells, scared to speak your mind, or need to make constant changes to accommodate their behaviours, this is not a healthy situation; it's abusive.

It may not be physical abuse, but this does not mean it doesn't cause you real harm and trauma. You may even be able to understand where the behaviour is stemming from; their upbringing or past relationship traumas for example. It is still NOT okay. It may be that you recognise they are not necessarily inflicting abuse on you purposefully or maliciously through conscious actions, but that is never an excuse and it is certainly no reason to stay.

You do not have to minimise or rationalise. You do not have to suffer in silence. You do not have to tolerate a situation that leaves you feeling as though you're afraid to be your authentic self, that you are tip toeing around someone, or that your freedom and choices are being restricted. There is a better way to live. There is help and support available. And you are not alone.

Cheryle Brown

Rejection

Right from the beginning I was rejected and a burden. My father happened to be there for the conception, but as it turns out was engaged to a nurse and was using my mother for what he could get.

My mother was an alcoholic before I was born. She remained so during the pregnancy and for years after I was born. My childhood was extremely lonely and confusing. My mother spent days and weeks in bed while my uncle looked after me. She self –harmed and tried to commit suicide numerous times and was admitted to psychiatric hospitals.

Some days I would wait outside school at home time for over an hour. Sometimes I'd wait longer, until eventually my uncle would collect me as my mother was passed out. I was excluded from playtime as I smelled and I was terrible at making friends; I always seemed to say or do the wrong thing.

My mother told me that I was cross just like my dad (who I'd never met and still haven't) and that I was useless and stupid like him, and she kept threatening to give me away. I grew up feeling numb, passive and over eager to please.

I left home aged eighteen to move in with a drug addict who was also an alcoholic. He beat me and raped me on a regular basis, which I felt like I deserved and thought that this was my lot in life. Every day he would tell me that I was fat, ugly, stupid and useless.

When I was twenty three I discovered that I was pregnant. Somehow I gathered the courage to get rid of him. I remained numb until I had my baby. Then suddenly, there was this little life looking to me for everything. I thought I was totally useless, but I knew I had to succeed at this. Little by little I ventured out to groups with my baby, and I discovered that I could communicate. I did it for my baby; this little person, the only person in the world who loved me and wanted me to be there. This was an alien sensation for me, but I loved it.

I began talking to a friend, and bit by bit I was able to reach the anger, hurt, rejection and pain within me by talking about things I had previously suppressed and deemed unimportant because I believed that I was unimportant. I began to see how I had come to this point. I could see that I had wanted to scream out for years: *this is wrong, this is not normal!*

I was so hurt by the years of want, neglect, mental torture, physical abuse and rejection, but now I can look back and know that I'm no longer there. I am now a wife and a mother to three beautiful children. I still fight with myself. I still find *fat, ugly, stupid* and *useless* circling in my mind, but I now recognise it as past pain; after all, knowledge is power.

****

My mother has been clean for seven years. She drank herself into oblivion for the last time the same number of years ago; she was unresponsive and just staring into space. She had not eaten in quite a while, not washed and had just given up waiting to die. I took her to Accident and Emergency where she was treated terribly before being admitted into a psychiatric hospital where she stayed for nine months. Slowly she began talking, moving about, and then after a few months could hold a conversation. Seven years on she has lasting damage in her body which will never heal, but although I maintain a guarded distance, she and I now have a relationship and she adores my children.

Alice

When Hurt People, Hurt People

The time I saw terror in my daughter's eyes was the time I woke up. I won't pretend that I'm now so enlightened that those shameful parenting moments no longer happen. But I will say that it awakened me to the damage we irrevocably cause our children, even with the best of intentions, when we don't examine and heal the wounds and unresolved trauma we received from our own childhood and adolescence.

I remember the time well. Ronnie was six weeks old, and suddenly his arrival hit Emilia, my then three-year-old, like a juggernaut. I was far from empathetic, expecting her to just 'get on with it' and accept her new baby brother when only a short time before she'd been the centre of my world. Love demonstrated via quality time and attention was the language she understood, but now I was largely ignoring her and pushing her away. Her behaviour deteriorated, and my egoic need to prove myself as being a 'good' parent who had it all under control - when I clearly didn't - was aggravated.

Then she hit me. And I saw red. And while I never hit her back, I did grab her - aggressively and non-consensually - and screamed in her face before carrying her over my shoulder up two flights of stairs, and throwing her on her bed. Yes, throwing- like I was discarding an unwanted toy.

As she stood there, sobbing and confused, pleading with me with her eyes not to hurt her, that's when I saw it. Pure terror. I'd frightened her. She was scared of me. The one person who was supposed to protect her had left her physically and emotionally vulnerable and unsafe.

And at that moment I saw my own inner child, the part of me who wanted nothing but love, affection and to feel safe, but who felt abandoned, scared, rejected and unloved. I remembered all those times in my own life when I'd felt that way throughout my childhood, adolescence and even early adulthood - memories that were buried so deep but never forgotten - and here I was allowing this vicious, fucked up co-dependent abuse cycle to continue.

Nothing prepares you for becoming a parent. Many of us have a romantic notion of what it will be like; a fantasy that we soon find rarely matches reality. I'm not suggesting that we shouldn't have children, and I'm certainly not demonising them. Kids are the most joyful and precious Beings. We can learn so much from their authenticity, their aptitude to love unconditionally and their presence. But what no one tells you is how emotionally triggering parenting can be, how children are often a mirror for our shadow, and how long-forgotten wounds creep to the surface before cracking wide open for the world to see. We feel vulnerable and exposed, masking the unwanted parts of ourselves to keep up the pretence that we've got it all figured out because God forbid anyone knew the truth.

Then we react to those wounds that were never ours to begin with, inherited from a long lineage of wounded adults before us. But by default of being a child, we took them on, the baggage getting heavier as we grew into adults before offloading onto our own children. And so the cycle continues.

Learning to Abuse

Children learn about relationships first by how they are treated, and second by what they observe in their environment. 'Do as I say, not as I do' is an adage that has never rung true. Treat a child respectfully, and they will learn to treat others respectfully. Treat them with kindness, and they will learn to treat others with kindness. Bully, coerce, manipulate, dismiss, gaslight, disrespect and use power 'over' to control a child and they'll learn that they don't matter, or that it's OK to treat others as they have been treated. And if we're honest, that's what many of us do. So often we hold our children to a much higher standard than we can uphold for ourselves, expecting them to behave mature, rational, respectful and kind, while we're unable to model those same behaviours.

I've said things and then on reflection realised how abusive those things were. I've emotionally pushed my kids away when what they needed was connection. I'm certainly not claiming to be a perfect parent - neither do I aspire to be - and neither am I sat here feeling sorry for myself and seeking reassurance and validation that 'I'm doing my best' and 'I'm a good mum'. Because at times I am not. At times, I am an arsehole, and I own that. I'm not using 'I'm doing the best I can with the resources I have' as a get-out-of-jail-free card because many times I've known better, yet in the height of reactivity have still chosen fear over love. We all have shitty parenting moments and we need to take responsibility for them instead of looking outwards for someone to blame or seeking validation that we're not a bad person really. The fact is, the victim-perpetrator dynamic that is entrenched in society has played out for centuries, and most of us have played both roles, including me.

So many of us fall into feeling parent shamed when we're called out for our behaviour when what we're experiencing is guilt; guilt because we know in our heart that we've behaved in a way that is harmful and wrong. It's time to take ownership of our guilt and use it to effect positive change. When you know better, you do better. It's a conscious choice. As is choosing to cause more harm even when you know it's wrong.

When I look into Ronnie's eyes, I see so much life and joy. When I look into Emilia's, I see a light that has dimmed. I'm very aware of the part I played in this; the ways that I haven't met her needs and the ways that I've perpetuated the abuse cycle, even when it was within my conscious control not to. Would I go back and do things differently? Of course. Hindsight is a beautiful thing! But I can't change the past. I can only step up and take responsibility to make amends now.

Children are very forgiving, and it's something we should never take for granted. They need to know that *yes*, we're human and we make mistakes, *yes* we can show empathy and compassion and recognise the pain of others BUT they need to know that they do not have to tolerate abuse, of any kind, from anyone, including their parents. No child should feel a duty of care or loyalty towards those who harm them, yet that's a pattern so easily learned in parent-child relationships. The lines between love and abuse get blurred. When I've apologised to Emilia in the past, and she's replied, 'that's okay', I made sure to tell her that 'no, it's *not* okay'. Children deserve to be treated with love, respect and kindness always, no matter what.

We all royally screw up from time-to-time and apologising is non-negotiable. You fuck up, you apologise. Don't listen to social dogma that tells you not to show weakness to your child, not to let them have the upper hand, not to cry in front of them and all that other bullshit. Apologise. Make amends. Demonstrate that adults are not always in the right, that adults get it wrong - very wrong - at times. Allow them to challenge your behaviour and call you out. Admitting your mistakes is strength, not a weakness. Every screw up is an opportunity to learn and commit to doing better. But repeating the same mistake and apologising for the same mistake over and over again doesn't cut it either.

When an ex-partner first hit me, I accepted his apology. Then it happened again. And again. I stayed with him for nearly three years; the physical abuse which 'only' happened on a few occasions - was nothing compared to the emotional abuse that stripped my confidence and spirit. It took a moment of insanity (or perhaps divine intervention?!) and me wrapping my hands tightly around his throat to realise how fucked up our relationship was. Only then did I leave, and only to keep *him* safe; never my own safety in mind!

We are taught what to tolerate. We are taught that we are responsible for other people's happiness - and rage. We are taught to be both complicit and submissive of abusive behaviour, not to make a fuss or speak up. We are taught to please and appease and 'be a good girl' at the expense of our own comfort and safety. We are taught to be victims (there is no victim-blaming here). And when our pain becomes unbearable, and we can no longer contain it, we turn into the perpetrator, physically or verbally unleashing it onto the weakest and most vulnerable: children.

When we fall into a pattern of yelling at our kids, emotionally detaching, withholding love and presence as punishment, spanking them or using shame or other oppressive means to control their behaviour, we are teaching them that abuse is okay. We are teaching them the kinds of behaviours to tolerate in future relationships. We are teaching them the types of relationships to expect and deserve. And we are teaching them that they are unworthy, undeserving and unlovable. Eventually, they stop loving themselves.

A child who stops loving themselves becomes an adult who doesn't love themselves and seeks unhealthy and destructive ways to self-medicate and fill the emptiness inside.

Abusive relationships. Alcohol dependency. Bulimia. Depression. Attempted suicide. Promiscuity. Toxic friendships. Anxiety. Self-sabotage. Self-neglect. And a pattern of self-destruction every time life is good because of a deeply entrenched belief that I'm not worthy or deserving of love. This is a summary of my story, the patterns of which still play out today, especially in those moments of unconscious parenting.

Breaking the Cycle

We'd be naive to think we can raise children free from pain. Pain and suffering are an inevitable part of the human experience. We can't always protect our children. We have no control over their experiences and the hurt that others may cause. But we can protect them from ourselves, which, uncomfortable as it is, is where their pain begins. There are no guarantees that our actions won't cause our children harm, no matter how conscious we are, but we can minimise the damage. We need to look inside ourselves and face our deepest, darkest, innermost wounds and be radically honest about the part we've played in enabling what is, for the most part, a deeply abusive culture.

We need to be honest about the ways we neglect and abuse ourselves and the dependency we place on others - our partners, friends and children - to fill the void. As much as we want to love our children unconditionally, few of us do. Our children are burdened by sets of rules and conditions to make them more acceptable and loveable, rules that we ourselves learnt and have carried down the lineage. No one taught us to love ourselves; we can't learn self-love from those who didn't love themselves either. But now we have the awareness, we can learn, and we can sow the seeds of self-love in our kids. The more we can instil a strong sense of self-love and worthiness in our children and model interdependence instead of co-dependency, the less likely they'll be to rely on others to give it to them. This does not mean that children raised in the happiest and healthiest of environments are immune from abuse: the dynamics are so insidious it can happen to anyone. But we need to be aware of the role that we, as parents play. And it starts with us. If we want to break the cycle and free our children from our pain, we need to do the work.

Stepping into a new parenting paradigm means unshackling ourselves from generations of pain, trauma and programming. It means removing the childist lens through which we have been indoctrinated to view children, and treating them with the respect, kindness and compassion that they deserve. Children don't have to earn their place in this world, they already belong. They don't owe us anything and shouldn't be punished for being born; for most of us, that was our choice. As is how we choose to treat them, moment to moment, even when it feels like we're losing control.

It starts with making a commitment to being the change and the person we needed as a child. It doesn't mean being the perfect parent or raising perfect kids. It doesn't mean you'll never screw up. But it does mean that when you do, you have the awareness to self-reflect, own your part, show yourself kindness and compassion, and move forward with grace.

Being a more 'conscious' parent is a daily practise, and not always an easy one because we all have our unconscious moments. It comes down to choice and re-committing daily to those choices. I can choose to raise my kids to live as the authentic expression of themselves, even the parts that challenge societal norms (and my own conditioning). I can choose to centre myself when they have an emotional meltdown and hold space regardless of who's watching or how I'm feeling. I can choose to recognise my triggers and prioritise my self-care so that they don't bubble over into my parenting. And I can choose to advocate for my kids, so they know that at least one person in their life has their back, no matter what.

Michelle Catanach

I Am Enough

Wait for someone special. Wait until you are of legal age. Don't give yourself to just anybody. These are the words I was given by my mother. Words with real intention.

I waited. Well, for the first two anyway. He was special. I was of age. But in hind sight he was just anybody. I was always proud of who I thought I was. I was the weird one who would make strange noises and flittered about day dreaming of being a lost boy in Neverland. I was happy. I didn't drink like most of my friends and I was sixteen years old, yet still possessed my virginity; a rarity in 2008. I had this idea in my head that if I waited until I was sixteen, and waited for the right boy, then I was doing it right. Little did I know the repercussions that would follow.

After a summer of house parties, big group outings, laughs and doing what all GCSE students do after exams, it all came to an abrupt end. I'm still not sure what I was expecting, or even wanting from him, but what I got sent me in to a spiral of darkness.

Towards the end of the summer he would say things like, "When are you going to look like Kiera Knightly?" And, "When are your boobs going to get smaller?" I was a busty size 8, I had never had an issue with my body before and I had never dieted. Suddenly I found myself smuggling my dinner to our family dog underneath the table, going days without eating and bringing my trusted Lucozade everywhere I went to give me energy. I was on a high. I lost weight and it soon became an obsession.

I once sat on the platform of the train station and watched a lady eating a sandwich. All I could think was *greedy, fat bitch. How can you eat that whole sandwich to yourself?!*

My days were a routine. Starve, binge, puke.

Then the darkness set in and the thought of being abandoned by this boy I had saved myself for hit hard.

Sleep.

It was my escape. But when I developed night terrors, my escape became terrifying, so I found myself taking prescription pills to numb this empty pain in my tummy. Tremadol. Zopliclone. Sleep.

A few months later I felt that nothing in this world would ever stop the pain that I felt. So, one morning before college, I wrote a letter to my mum and dad. I told them that it would be better if I was no longer here to be a burden on the family. I explained that I couldn't live without that boy and that I'd be happier permanently asleep.

I put the letter underneath their bed and travelled to college with a pack of Tremadol in my bag. Before my first lesson of that day, I took the pills and headed to my theatre class. Very shortly after I felt my brain beginning to fuzz. I felt relief that soon I could sleep. Suddenly, my mum and dads faces came into my mind. I didn't think I was worthy enough to break their hearts. I thought they would live the rest of their lives angry with me. I panicked. I told my closest friend in that class and he quickly informed my tutor. I became more aware of my surroundings when I arrived at A&E in the ambulance. The doors opened, and there stood my mum with tears rolling down her blotchy face. A paramedic looked at her and reassured her that I did it for attention.

All I wanted to do was scream that I wanted to die. How dare this man say it was for attention! I didn't want to wake up from the nightmare I believed I was living; the constant fight I had with myself on a daily basis. The utter hatred I had for myself and for him who I thought was responsible for all of this. They forced the very little food I had inside straight out of me, along with a concoction of Lucozade and pills. My body was alive. But I was dead inside.

I was not to be trusted to travel to school on my own. I was sent to the Child and Adolescent Mental Health unit for regular sessions. I had to do questionnaires to calculate how much I wanted to die. My scores were high. I found myself listening to the same depressing songs on repeat. *Stepping Stone* by Duffy and *Russian Roulette* by Rhianna. I guess I was drawn to others who felt the way I did.

For nearly two years I woke abruptly in the night- three or four times- screaming at the top of my lungs, swimming in a pool of sweat. My dad would run in, put his hand on my head and stay until I quickly fell asleep again.

I left that school year innocent and happy with the world at my feet. I came back after the summer with a dark cloud following me everywhere I went, with no real chance to escape it. No longer was I the weird, upbeat, random girl. I was the sad one. The one who's true smile was a distant memory.

The pills were hidden, but the doctor gave me more. Although I still didn't want to be here, I found something that gave me hope. *The Secret*. Positive thinking that will change your life. And it did. The self-help book written by Rhonda Byrne discusses the idea of the Law of Attraction, suggesting that your thoughts manifest into reality. So, I began to day dream of the actress I wanted to be. The stages where I'd perform. The film sets I would call home. The different characters I could be. Anything but be me!

Ten years have passed since I first felt worthless, unwanted, rejected and alone, but now I would never want to be anyone but me. I love me. I love every inch of the skin I wear. I love every freckle, every roll, every bruise, but most importantly I love my mind.

I am in love with how positive I am. How I see the good in every situation. How I want the best for everyone I meet. How I want my nearest and dearest to be the best versions of themselves because I am living proof that there is always a reason to live. I don't have an ounce of negativity in me towards that boy. He is just another stranger now, who I would greet with the same compassion I would anyone else. I don't like to think ugly thoughts about anybody now, all it does is make you feel bad in yourself.

I haven't stepped foot on a stage in five years. I have no need to because the life I have now is better than any character I could ever portray.

Hannah Charlton

This. Is. My. Truth.

I have spent many hours pondering how to express my story, or at least some of it, writing and rewriting over again. I guess the question I kept asking is *where do I start?* Or perhaps more importantly *when did it begin?* Truthfully, I have no idea; there are so many moments in my life that filled Pandora's Box, and it's only now that I am in my thirties that I am sifting through the contents. This is not a journey I wanted to take, but it's one that I need to. And the reality is this: once Pandora's Box opens, there is no going back.

I spent most of my life screaming loudly and wondering why no one could hear me, why no one saw my pain, and why no one noticed the signs that I was hurting. And then one day it finally hit me; no one could hear me because my screams were silent; screams that echoed through my body and vibrated through my soul but which made no sound for others to hear. My truth screamed silently and so my pleas for help were inaudible, my pain and abuse invisible.

I cannot recall the exact day I first started hating myself, or cutting myself, or the first time I wanted to end my life, or even the first time I attempted suicide. There are so many moments, remembering the first is a bit of a blur. But I do know that nothing exacerbated my anguish more than Pandora's Box exploding open!

There is something so real about your truth finally being spoken out loud; it took me the best part of three decades to face it and reveal all to the world (which I did by writing a chapter in a book). It was a massive release to tell someone, to tell everyone that I am a sexual abuse survivor. And I am that; a survivor! I named the ghosts in my darkness and shed light where none had shone before; it was liberating in so many ways, and I am so grateful for those who have supported me throughout this journey. What I didn't expect was the aftermath of sharing such deep truths. I had not expected my childhood to come flooding back to me in a tsunami of never-ending flashbacks, nightmares and memories. I was so utterly overwhelmed and began to wonder why I even existed. *What was my purpose and why bother with it?*

I often wished I could just disappear and that would be the end of it. Writing that chapter had freed me in so many ways, but with Pandora's Box now well and truly open, there was no way of stopping the contents from pouring out.

I am not going to sit here and lie and say I have handled it well. I haven't, and life isn't a bed of roses. I have been to the bottom of the dark hole and back for what seems like the hundredth time in my life. I have revisited my old friend and my enemy: self-harm. I have begged for my life to end, to stop, and for it all to go away. I have hit the self-destruct button. This is not the first time in my life that I have been here, but it is the first time I have genuinely asked myself if this is what I REALLY want, or whether perhaps there is another way? And it is the first time I have been open and honest about what that is: inner peace. But each time I think I am beginning to reach that place, I find another layer that needs peeling back and I find myself back at the beginning. The process of healing is never an easy one.

It wasn't until recently that I truly knew the extent of my sexual abuse, which I'd perhaps blocked out, and with this realisation, my world imploded around me. And it was at this time that I also realised the scope of the damage caused not just by my childhood sexual abuse, but by my childhood in general. And yes, I use the word damage; it's not that I am damaged, but there was damage caused by living a life silently screaming inside. When the veil lifts, you begin to see with crystal sharp clarity how fucked up things were growing up, and how fucked up it can all still now be because you hold on to those conditions of childhood.

As I sit here writing this, I can recall distinct times in my childhood that have had a profound effect on my life both then and now, and not all in a positive way. Some of these moments have shaped a very warped existence, both in how I feel inside and with how I interact with the external world. They have been beliefs that have contributed to many broken relationships and have created a parallel reality where I am neither this person nor that. I am only what I choose to show you, all the while breaking inside.

The abuse started when I was a toddler. It is almost as if I had no hope with my mental health from the get-go. Growing up I was different from others.

Outwardly I appeared confident, yet locked the real me inside, protected from the world. At junior school I went through the motions, but withdrew more and more as I got older, plagued with insecurities, exhaustion, confusion, rage and self-loathing. Ironically, all of this isolation and self-loathing came not long after the abuse stopped. I mean, how messed up is that?! I'd experienced abuse from such a young age that it felt normal and I believed that this is what was done. And then one day, when it just suddenly stopped, I was left confused; there was a mixture of relief and rejection. I breathed a sigh of liberation but equally held onto that breath, wondering what was wrong with me. *Why was I no longer lovable?* How fucked up is sexual abuse? That a child is made to confuse abuse with love and self -worth?

When I reached my early teenage years the moments that affected my self-esteem became more and more apparent. One of these moments was the night my mom and dad's argument got so out of control, and so violent, that I feared my mom would die. Even writing this here in black and white, I can feel the fear building, the tears wanting to cascade down my cheeks. I can hear myself screaming for it all to stop. I can still hear their voices, the shouting. I can smell the fear and see the rage building. I can still feel time standing still and hear my heart pounding in my ears. This was the moment I intervened in their fight, the moment that I threw a paperweight at my dad. I can still see his face when he turned to look at me; the hatred and the rage. Even as I write this I am thinking, *shit, I am in for the hiding of a lifetime here*. He didn't hit me, well not that I can recall, and the fighting stopped. That night was the first time I distinctly remember wanting my life to end, but not knowing how to do it. Despite being physically alive, a piece of me did die that night anyway.

In addition to all the other emotional baggage stuffed into my box, I now carried the burden of feeling responsible for my mother and sister. The events that followed that night were a mixture of survival, escape and acceptance. This is the time I developed my best coping mechanism: sleep. And still, to this day when things are emotionally too much for me, I have an intense urge to go to bed and sleep and sleep and sleep. Nothing is different when I am awake, but sleeping is as close to dying as I can get.

Fast forward a few traumatic years, and I had a basket full of coping mechanisms which included self-harming, drinking, smoking, sleeping (a lot), self-pleasure (which only bought with it more feelings of shame, guilt and self-hatred) and OCD. And yet no one noticed. No one noticed that I had given up sports, that I had put on weight and was deeply unhappy with my body, that I was more provocative than someone of my age should be, that I was manipulative with boys and that I was broken. My behaviours became a physical demonstration of my silent screams and still no one heard me!

We eventually moved to a new country, just my mom, my sister and me, and it wasn't long after we got to the UK that I attempted suicide for the first time. It was my lowest point, and I couldn't see a way out. I took a load of pills with an excessive amount of alcohol hoping never to wake up. I did. I remember feeling like death for days and hating myself even more. I felt like a failure. I started self-harming more and more – and with each cut, I could feel the pain, the shame and the ugliness seeping out of my body. When I did eventually tell someone I was hurting myself, I couldn't explain the messed -up emotions that led to it, and I was accused of attention seeking. This made me retreat further into myself.

It did get to a point where physically hurting myself wasn't enough, and the rage that was building needed a new outlet. By my twenties, I had well and truly hit the self-destruct button. I had attempted suicide three times. I had cutting myself down to a fine art. And I was giving sex away in a very controlled and manipulative manner to whomever I chose. Sex had become a game, something that didn't involve feeling but more of an ego boost. I was crap at everything else in life, but this I could control - who, when, where - and whether or not I made them fall in love with me. Men became disposable in the same way I had been, not only with the abuse but within other aspects of family life too. The partying lifestyle had led me to drink more and sometimes with people I hardly knew but wanted so badly to trust. During one of of these nights I was date raped. I never reported it because I believed that girls like me deserve it. I had gotten myself into that situation and falsely believed that I had been in control. I HATED myself. And I HATED everyone around me for not seeing my pain.

In my early to mid-twenties I began looking at myself from a different perspective, as if through a looking glass. I needed to change, to get help, to talk to someone. And I did. Firstly, I visited my GP who, to be honest, didn't do much. But then I spoke to a friend, who was all kinds of amazing. She got it, she really did. And for a while, I was doing ok. I was exercising more as my release, drinking less and no longer socially smoking. I began to explore other avenues to deal with my depression, rage and shame, shedding light on the darkness within.

I was functioning. I had an amazing job. I was on track. And I was starting to find out who I truly am. By this point, I was married to a very supportive man, who has brought both the dark and the light out of me (that's another chapter). But, as I have come to realise in my life, the good is often followed by a BUT, and in this case, we experienced three miscarriages. Old feelings began to resurface. By the time we did fall pregnant again I was already down the rabbit hole with my old friends; shame, guilt and failure, with even more indistinguishable feelings joining the party. I held it together for the pregnancy. Then came the birth, which was one of the most traumatic experiences I have ever had. That day I was violated all over again. Not one person in that room asked for my permission. Not one person asked for consent to examine, touch, or use forceps. Not one person listened to me! I remember screaming at them and watching their faces as they ignored me. Once again, the familiar feeling of invisibility resurfaced. No one heard me except for my husband, and in his defence, they weren't listening to him either.

I suffered from Post Natal Depression (PND); something that isn't talked about and in my case also very much linked to the trauma I had experienced as a child. I didn't know it then, but the pot was beginning to boil over. I didn't do much about my PND. I wasn't diagnosed until I was pregnant with my second child, but the signs were there. I rarely left the house. I cried a lot. I felt like a complete failure, and I couldn't cope most of the time and had no real reason for it. I wanted to just throw it all in, to walk away, but I couldn't leave this helpless little bundle. Now looking back, I know the birth experience triggered my abuse memories and therefore the descent into the shadows.

This was five years ago, and since then I have had another baby and have been on the biggest roller coaster ride of my life. I have been so low that I have not been able to get out of bed for days. I have been so tired and sleep deprived from nightmares, flashbacks and fears. I went through a period where I couldn't sleep at all if my husband was working (he works shifts), and even now if he is working late, I don't sleep well at all. My weight has yo-yoed; either I am healthy and loving life, or my inner critic is there and I do everything I can to silence her through food. I have pulled myself away from friends because I do not have the energy to be and to do anymore. I stopped going out and focused on my home life; me, my kids.

I have been very destructive in my relationship with my husband, and by destructive, I mean self-sabotaging; expecting the worst all the time and when I don't get the worst, I almost create it, so my inner child can say, 'See, I told you!'

In an eighteen- month period I had to watch my daughter go to hell and back, similar in many ways to my own experiences, and I felt broken and enraged. I wanted cycles to be broken, my silence to be heard and my daughter to have the voice I never did. I no longer wanted to be ashamed of me, and that meant all of me; my mental health along with all the dirty secrets. That was when I decided to write my story about my abuse and co-authored a book. Who knew that when the book was released it would cause so much emotion, flashbacks and memories to rush to the surface like a torrential downpour?

The months since the book was released have been the hardest ever. I have felt like giving up and have been so low I have been nothing but numb, or just so full of tears that I have cried for hours. I have felt like a complete failure and that my family would be better off without me, but I am still here, and I am still fighting. Sometimes it feels that I'm barely winning the battle, but my heart is still beating. I won't give up because I don't want this to be my story. There is no way in hell my past is going to win, and this fuels me.

As I sit here typing, I wonder if I was so overwhelmed by my revelation because every floodgate opened at once and EVERYTHING came rushing out of my box at full speed. In the past I'd never really addressed my pain, just used behaviours which helped to mask it because I lived in fear of speaking my truth. I felt vulnerable and overwhelmed that the contents of my very own Pandora's Box were out there for everyone to see. Knowing that I needed to finally confront my fears, my wounds and my past, I decided to see my GP. They were as useful as a chocolate teapot, but I wanted a referral. They offered me anti-depressants. I am not against anti-depressants, especially as I am on them now, but I wanted another way that didn't numb me. At this point I was really growing spiritually, so I decided to try a Homeopath to help stabilise my moods. This was a life saver.

I found a therapist and got talking. And then randomly one day I entered a competition and won some life coaching sessions with an amazing kick-ass woman. She talked me off the ledge so many times metaphorically speaking and the questions she asked really got me thinking about ME and what I wanted. This was a huge turning point. I started looking at people around me and asking whether that person deserved to be in my life and started living my truth, unashamed and unapologetically (this is still very much a work in progress). I wrote my story. I told the world. I was no longer willing to remain silently screaming my truth.

And today I am sharing this with you to show you that you are not alone, that you have no reason to be ashamed and to use your rage to fuel your fire and fight your fight. To be you - unapologetically - and fuck everyone else!

Crystle Jones

Courage

Courage Doesn't Need to Roar 61

Cancer and PTSD 66

Life is Not a Destination 71

Denial of Pain 74

Inside I Am Screaming 77

Miscarriage 82

It twists inside 85

Coming Full Circle 86

The Lie You Sold 89

Drowning on the Inside 91

Running 97

A Self-Portrait 99

Women Together 104

Echoes 105

Finding Balance 105

Who Am I? 107

Courage Doesn't Need to Roar

Whoever told you motherhood is easy, is lying. I knew it would be hard, but the complexity of changes, both emotional and physical, is something none of us are ever really prepared for. Antenatal classes prepare us for labour, birth and how to care for a new baby, but no one ever really teaches you how to look after yourself. How not to lose yourself or your identity when you become a mother. There are so many systems in place to safeguard our beautiful children and babies, but when was the last time someone asked you how you are? How you *really* are? Why is it that once baby is here, the mother is forgotten?

Don't get me wrong, I love being a mother; it's the most rewarding experience I could have ever imagined. My mother always told me, "You will only understand when you are a mother." And it's true. No words can do it justice, but it's opened my eyes to a whole new world. Where does the reality lie? Is it somewhere between the mothers I see, as patients, in tears at my door because they feel they are failing as a parent -that mother I once was- and the social media mother who has it all together, with the beautiful breastfeeding shots and the slim, perfectly recovered postpartum body? The pressure we put upon ourselves as women and mothers, the expectations we create unknowingly, is the most unhealthy thing we can do to ourselves.

Being pregnant the first time round I was surrounded by these beautiful photos of love at first sight between mother and baby after birth. There's the perfect birth plan and books full of advice on how to 'sleep train' your baby, how much to feed your baby, and pages and pages of contradicting advice like 'cuddle more, but don't cuddle too much'. When did we lose our innate intuition as mothers and replace it with 'evidence based' books by 'experts' telling us how to raise children that we, as women, have been doing for thousands of years? I remember the exhaustion I felt after a twelve hour labour and I remember the relief I felt when the pain stopped and she was delivered, but what sticks in my mind the most is when they handed her to me... that expectation of overwhelming love and tears was met with nothing but fear. *I can't do this, I don't know how to do this.* Everything I had been taught, read, learnt was leading up to this point, but no one can tell you what comes next. This wasn't like the photos, the stories or the blogs. *It wasn't meant to be like this,* I kept thinking to myself.

I will admit, I was caught up by it all, even though I promised myself I wouldn't be. But after having my first daughter, I found myself hating what I saw in the mirror looking back at me. I cried at pre-pregnant photos of myself and questioned my mothering skills. My body wasn't the same, the pregnancy glow had worn off no matter how much I tried to glam myself back up and I ended up hating myself more. *Why wasn't my baby sleeping the recommended six hours in the day, or drinking the exact 120mls recommended every three hours?* I'd failed myself and my body, but why was I failing her too?

Being told by professionals, who were meant to be there for support in those difficult early days, that I should supplement my breastfeed with formula because I had a 'small' baby, despite her gaining weight, was a hard pill to swallow. I remember leaving in tears. She had just confirmed my fear:
I'm not enough.

Once baby was out, the baby was all that mattered. The broken body hiding beneath the clothes was something no one wanted to know about or talk about. You were a mother now, 110% devoted to this tiny human you'd grown inside you for nine months. But where are you? The person you were before baby? That person isn't what's looking back at you in the mirror. I remember thinking, *I don't even recognise me anymore.*

Maternity leave was hard. I felt isolated and alone. The continuous sense of dependence from this tiny baby was terrifying and exhausting, mentally, physically and emotionally. You end up questioning yourself, *how did our mothers do it, our grandmothers, great grandmothers?* But we forget. Previous generations' babies were raised in communities, by neighbours, by aunts, by relatives, friends and elders in a close-knit society. Not in this 21st century world where everything is time dependent, technology dependent, photo dependent, social media dependent. What we've achieved through the will to communicate is losing physical touch, losing communities for our children and ultimately isolating ourselves. Nothing can replace that, no matter how advanced the technology.

For me, I found myself a new me, when I returned to work as a GP. I had a completely new insight; I now understood mothers and babies. I understood and empathised, but with a real connection and not in the way I naively had pre-motherhood. My practice changed. My first question to a mother and baby I would see in clinic was, "How is mummy?" Instead of my previous, "How is baby?" I remember wishing that everyone would notice me more instead of heading straight to baby. I remember wishing someone would notice the brave front I wore to the world, instead of asking the standard questions driven by society's expectations:

"Are you still breastfeeding?"

"Does baby sleep through the night yet?"

"Are they babbling, crawling, talking yet?"

"Maybe you should interact with them more, take them to more classes."

And yet we still wonder with all this pressure, demand and expectation society creates on new mothers, why the rates of antepartum and postpartum depression have risen exponentially in the last decade.

My ten minute consultations turned into thirty, with me repeating:

"You are enough."

"Fed is best."

"Stop putting so much pressure on yourself, use your support network."

"Take a break, go for a walk, alone."

"You are everything that baby needs."

Over and over and over again. And it hit me – the words I wished I had been told, wished I had told myself. The words I wished I could have believed. The Mum guilt is real, but it was created by the demands of a society that envisages a devoted mother as one that never leaves their child, stays home and gives 110% of herself, 150% of the time. But taking time out to breathe, to take care of you, is not selfish. It's the bravest thing you can do for you both. You need to be in a good place, to look after you, to be able to be the best version of yourself for your child. You both deserve that.

You need to find your own identity, to be able to guide your child to grow and find theirs. They say put on your own oxygen mask before you can help others in an emergency, so learn to breathe.

Motherhood isn't a picture, a book, a guide or a staged photo. It's a connection. A connection to other mothers, our children, our partners, family, friends and the rest of the world. We are the real-life role models for our sons, our daughters. How we see ourselves is how they will learn to self-reflect. How we feel within ourselves will reflect in our interaction with them, and teach the next generation to come. So be kind to yourselves, to each other. Put five minutes aside each day to breathe, to notice the beauty in right now, in yourself. Your body may not be what it was, but each scar you see, every stretch mark on your wounded body tells a story. It shows a life well lived, survived, an imperfect beauty that makes you unique from the monotonous social media "glam". Create your own kind of beautiful. Embrace the imperfections, for that is real beauty.

And even as I say this, I have faced the same self-loathing again, if not worse, with my second pregnancy. But I will be kinder this time. I am different, I am stronger, I am still me, but also a mother. I will embrace this change and be braver this time, because love needs to start within yourself. And yet I keep whispering to myself... *it's OK, I'm allowed to feel this way, this is real life.*

Courage doesn't need to roar. It's the tiny whisper telling me to keep trying, keep loving, keep believing. Because the only thing guaranteed in life is change. If we don't embrace it, we lose the most precious thing we have in this world... time. I want my daughters to look at me and see my scars, my imperfections, my stretch marks and to hear my stories.

This is real life. This is the everlasting beauty within us all.

Dr Sahar Jahanian

Cancer and PTSD

The hardest thing I ever had to do was tell my children that I had cancer. On that day I believed that nothing could hurt more than tearing a huge hole in the safety blanket of my family. I was wrong. The hardest thing I've ever had to do was survive the emotional fallout resulting from my diagnosis.

I was forty two years old, relatively fit and healthy, not overweight, a non-smoker and only rarely drank alcohol when I felt something abnormal in the base of my right breast. My immediate thought was that it was cancer and that I was going to die. Then followed my GP referral, clinic appointments, mammograms, ultrasounds, biopsies, more biopsies and finally confirmation on 26th November 2014 that it was breast cancer. Just five short weeks between my discovery and the surgery that undoubtedly saved my life.

Five long weeks during which I could feel the lump growing.

Five weeks during which my life changed forever.

The time following diagnosis takes on a life of its own, as you follow the treatment regime from week to week. Life becomes singularly focused as, scared and anxious, you move along the cancer conveyor belt. There's no future vision beyond the next appointment, plans are cancelled and your treatment becomes your whole world.

You are no longer living, but simply existing in a state of constant stress and fear.

One year on

November 2015, one year into my eighteen months of treatment and I was back in the breast clinic for my first annual mammogram and check-up. I was terrified. From the moment I opened the appointment letter I felt certain that they would find cancer in my remaining breast and I would have to go through surgery and chemotherapy again. I could hardly breathe as I sat in the waiting room, trembling, my heart pounding. I felt sick and dizzy. I didn't want to know. I couldn't go through it all again.

I was fortunate in that the consultant was available in clinic to review my mammogram straight away. When she told me it was clear I asked, "Are you sure?" Three times I checked that she was certain my mammogram showed no abnormalities. Finally, believing her, I felt my body and mind release all the stress that had been building for twelve months, and for the first time I thought that maybe I'd be ok.

How wrong I was.

Within days I was drowning in a tidal wave of depression. It's difficult to describe exactly how I felt other than to say that nothing mattered anymore; there was no present, there was no future, just a blank void in which I was trapped. I struggled with every aspect of life.

I felt worthless.

Hopeless.

Helpless.

And completely alone.

I shut down. I felt numb. The world around me was still living, but it felt like everything was out of focus and muffled. I felt disconnected from reality. My every breath pointless.

I couldn't ask for help, I didn't know how. I couldn't pick up the phone. I couldn't let anyone know exactly how bad I felt. My mind flitted between hope and despair, with conflicting thoughts that tomorrow would be better and dread that tomorrow would be just the same, over and over.

Weeks drifted into months and things weren't getting better despite anti-depressants, despite counselling, despite my continual efforts to make myself well. Active treatment finished, my second annual mammogram was clear, and for the third year Christmas passed me by.

In May 2017 I had an assessment appointment with psychology. Following this I was told that the reason I wasn't recovering from my depression was because I wasn't only dealing with depression, but had post-traumatic stress disorder (PTSD) as well.

I didn't understand. I thought PTSD was something soldiers had from experiencing war. My psychologist explained how my symptoms fit with a diagnosis of PTSD, and after a few appointments I started to understand more about how it was affecting me. I began to recognise triggers that would bring on physical reactions, or intrusive memories. I learnt new ways of managing my symptoms. And with an intensive therapy called EMDR, I began to process the trauma which was causing me to feel this way.

My story doesn't end there.

Being diagnosed with cancer has given me an awareness of the fragility of life; there is no guarantee of ongoing good health or a long life. We don't know what the future holds and can't influence fate or destiny. All we can do is live the best version of our life.

I will always be someone who had cancer, the person who detonated a bomb in the middle of their family. I have lost over three years of my life through treatment and the emotional limbo that resulted from my diagnosis. But with therapy and anti-depressants, with a lot of support from my GP and with my own commitment to recovery, I have relearnt how to live.

Karen Horsley

Life is not a Destination

Things are much better than they once were, but this battle is a journey that will last a lifetime. I didn't think I would get this far, and to be honest I'm not always glad I have. I have no choice but to be a fighter, but this also means I find it hard to show my vulnerability for fear I may be hurt; my battle makes me far more aware that I need to protect myself. Who's going to stand up for me if I don't?

There was a time I only wanted to self-destruct, a period that lasted the best part of a decade. This chaos led to an abrupt ending of my school years with no goodbyes, something which I have never quite come to terms with and still feel sad about. My memory is hazy of this time, but I know I spent most of these years in and out of psychiatric wards, desperately self-harming and attempting suicide. I've no idea how many attempts I have made, there are too many to remember. And I cannot tell you how many of these were genuine 'I want to be dead for good, I do not want to be saved' and how many were 'cries for help'; desperate attempts to stop the roaring pain inside of me, and to be heard when I wasn't being listened to, or simply could not express myself. Many of those attempts were very much life threatening though, and by law of probability, I doubt I should be here now.

The scars inside of me are far worse than the scars I wear on my arms; I was wounded by my experiences, my attempts to survive them and by the medical treatment attempting to save me. Both my body and mind took a battering through my years of self-abuse. I sometimes feel my physical scars mark me out as defective; I feel ashamed and fearful that they leave me exposed to be judged, but the truth is that they are my battle scars that show how strong I am, as opposed to how weak. I am a warrior. If I hadn't self-harmed, I doubt I'd have coped, and would have probably successfully committed suicide. I simply didn't have the strategies necessary back then to cope with the pandemonium of my mind. In present day moments of pain and depression I am not always glad I have survived, but mostly I am, as I would have also missed the good things life has offered.

My experiences have given me a unique insight; I can see the suffering in people where some can't, and I have compassion for that. It pains me to think of someone suffering without a voice, like I once was, and I am willing to be their voice if I can. Inside psychiatric hospitals, it was very disturbing at times, but the patients were some of the most amazing people I have met, showing true kindness to each other during the worst moments of their lives.

I didn't realise I had Asperger syndrome, or autism, until I was diagnosed aged thirty two. I was initially diagnosed with Borderline / Emotionally Unstable Personality Disorder, alongside eating disorders when I was younger. Not knowing I had Asperger's meant I wasn't able to understand myself properly. I can now understand myself on a much deeper level; at the foundations I have Asperger syndrome, and this is the way my brain is wired. And then I have the mental health issues layered on top of that. Asperger's makes you more prone to mental health issues. I have always struggled with the Personality Disorder diagnosis, as it feels such a condemning label, with such negative perceptions attached. I feel it's led to some very punitive and dismissive treatment by both medical and psychiatric professionals in the past, and I still question whether the diagnosis fits me or not.

It wasn't until I stopped running and learned to care for myself, that I found some relief from my chaos. I try not to see danger everywhere I look, but my anxiety and experiences can make me hyper vigilant. I have tried to come off medication numerous times, as I find the side effects hard to cope with, but I can't stay well without it. My default mode when stressed still seems to be to have suicidal thoughts, but I now have the wisdom and the knowledge to know that 'this too shall pass'.

I struggle to find my place in the world. I don't have a successful career, a significant other, or children to be proud of; I wish society didn't use these things to define people, as this makes me feel very inferior. I have the love I give, and that is me. I am not going to pretend everything's okay; life's a struggle, but I live it as much as I'm able to and I'm safe. My pain is no longer raw. I have found relief through the beautiful children who have touched my life and brought me some of the purest joy. I have been grounded by my pets, especially my precious little dog, whom I owe so much to; he brings me so much reassurance and comfort, makes me laugh every day and gives me the freedom to go out when I feel too anxious to go alone.

Keeping well for me is all about the basics: a balance of diet, exercise, fresh air, sleep, medication, routine, social contact, solitude and of course wisdom. Mindfulness and meditation really help when I feel motivated enough to practice them! When the dark times come, then maintaining the basics is even more crucial to surviving and it is how I cope, as well as being extra gentle with myself. I acknowledge that I will probably get ill again, but I know the signs, so I am able to act quickly. I can admit that I have made mistakes and will again, but life is a journey and not a destination.

Hannah March

Denial of pain is always easier than facing it.

But no one ever discovered their full potential by taking the easy road.

Inside I Am Screaming

I have MS. Multiple Sclerosis. There has been demyelination in my body across time and space. It still feels new to me, even though more than a year has passed since my diagnosis, but of course MS isn't new to me: it has been in my body for some time, but it is only recently that my conscious mind has become aware of it. That might mean that the fatigue symptoms I attributed to PTSD hypo-crash, or the falling over that I attributed to clumsiness, were MS too. But we'll never know. And it doesn't matter. What matters now, is that I have a disease, the prognosis of which is a mystery even to the expert neurologists who research it.

Having MS means that the time of the next relapse and which new symptoms it might bring, and how intense and life-limiting they might be, is unknown. Every day there isn't a relapse is a blessing. And also, every night I go to bed not knowing if tomorrow will be a day where I wake up blind, or with a limb or limbs paralysed. These are extremes, but they might happen. If they happen, they might last minutes, or hours. Or they might last weeks or months, or never pass at all. I am waiting for the time when my arm decides to spasm and throws a glass of wine in my date's face.

MS is a snowflake disease. And with all the other connotations of snowflake, it is a word I am content to adopt. It's a snowflake disease, not because we are fragile or weak, but because it shows up differently in every person who has it. No two MS diagnoses have the same symptoms, and there is no prognosis of what will happen, or when. When I was first diagnosed, I was told I should expect to need a wheelchair within ten years. But that might never happen. Or it might happen tomorrow.

You can't see that I have MS. Sometimes, when my body is tired, you might notice a limp in my walk, dragging one leg. If you look closely, you might notice a twitch in my hand. You might see me hold my thigh or stroke my calf – but you won't know that it is because I am trying to soothe the pain. You won't see the spiders crawling on my legs. You won't see the electric shocks zapping randomly across my body. You won't see the pins and needles that can come on so fast and mean I feel frozen, unable to remember how to move my legs. You won't see the hours I sleep when the fatigue hits, or the corset I am wearing when the MS hug constricts my breathing. My lived experience is invisible. You can't see I have MS.

I try to take it one day at a time, being grateful for the limited symptoms that I have now, in the knowledge that one day they might be far less manageable. Mindfulness and meditation are a daily practice; to stay in the now. I also reflect daily on other things I am grateful for and mitigate my fears for the future, which must not become overwhelming, even when they feel suffocating.

When brain fog creeps in, or I'm wading through treacle and the words on the screen seem to be floating and unanchored, it serves no purpose for me to give into the terror of when I won't be able to earn my own living and will be dependent on the state system, and the difficulties in making ends meet that will entail. Losing my financial independence is terrifying, but the screams inside must never take over.

When I've been walking around town and my legs move ever more slowly and feel ever more heavy, or when I've spent a couple of nights up late having fun, I am made to pay with the driving need for sleep regardless of what else it means I'm missing. Or when I drop the jar I was trying to open, it serves me no purpose to give into the terror of when I won't be able to look after myself and imagine that wheelchair, the inability to cook for myself, to wash myself, to wipe my bum. Losing my physical independence is terrifying, and the screams inside must be shushed or they will paralyse me before I am paralysed.

I am single, I have no partner to care for me. I have no children to care for me. I have debts, not savings. I have no safety net for when MS becomes unmanageable. The screams inside grow louder.

Inside I am screaming and my job everyday is to acknowledge those screams, not ignore them or push them down, but to lean in and accept them. And at the same time, not allow them to overwhelm me, not let them pull me into feeling victimised, not let them make me a martyr, not let them define me. My relationship with my MS is the most complex relationship I've ever been in. I must learn to be in partnership with it, not fight it. I do not want to be a warrior fighting my MS. I am lover, mother and queen making room for MS to be part of my everyday experience, welcoming in the MS, as it will do as it pleases anyway.

I am screaming inside because I have MS and MS hurts. And when you show pity for me, when you tell me it's not fair that I have MS, when you are trying to find the words to show your sympathy for me and you say it shouldn't be happening to me, I scream inside. I do not want your pity. I do not want your sympathy. Don't make me into someone to feel sorry for. Do not take away my agency. Do not see me as victim.

I am screaming inside because I have MS and when the next relapse will happen is a mystery, and that is terrifying. And when you tell me to be strong, when you say these things happen and the only thing to do is accept it, I scream inside. I am being as strong as I know how, and it is tiring to be working all the time on my attitude and response to MS, as well as the background symptoms, as well as the normal everyday angst of being human. Do not dismiss my pain, my battle that I am waging whether I want to or not, by telling me to be strong. Yes, these things do happen. But do not dismiss my experience of this thing happening with platitudes to make you feel better.

I am screaming inside because I have MS and I have a big vision for changing the world, and being of service to empower others to change their worlds too. And when you tell me that this is fate, my destiny, those of us who are meant for big things are always challenged by the universe, and this is just that challenge for me to prove my worthiness and determination to achieve my dreams, I scream inside. No. The universe did not give me MS to test my worthiness. I do not need to be worthy, or unworthy, to achieve my dreams. MS is frickin' inconvenient in my efforts to make those dreams come true, but it didn't happen because the universe wants to test my faith. It just happened and it just is.

I am screaming inside because when you ask me how I am, I am not fine. And I don't want to deny my own experience by telling you that I am fine, and I don't want to be the person who is always telling you why I am not fine. I don't want to bring my symptoms to the forefront by talking about them and I don't want to live a life where I am forever complaining about my symptoms. They just are. And I am not fine. If I tell you about all the other things that are making me happy, or unhappy, without also telling you about how the MS is showing up, it does not mean it isn't there. It is always there. When you ask me how I am, I do not know how to answer.

Inside, I am screaming. And yet, there is no way to make you understand. I can talk about it, share what is happening, refuse to be shamed by the symptoms that mean I need to express my needs and not take on a mantle of victimhood whilst doing so, but there is no way to make you understand. Because you don't have MS. And, even more, you don't have my version of MS. So, however I try to communicate what it is, it is invisible. I am unseen. Being unseen is isolating, lonely, hurtful. There is a distance now between us that seems fated to always be there.

You cannot get it right. And I cannot express to you what I need from you because I do not know what I need from you. And the distance between us becomes a chasm.

Inside, I am screaming.

Emily Jacob

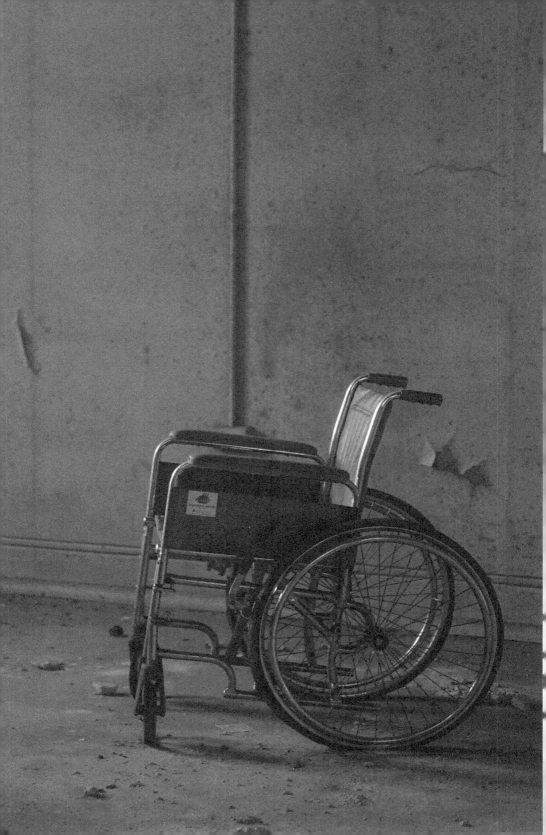

I just couldn't stop crying; ALL of the time. In the street. At dinner. In the supermarket. A wave of deep sadness would just wash over me, and I couldn't control my tears. After a few weeks, people kept telling me that I should be feeling better by now, that I needed to 'get over it'. But I didn't know how to 'get over it'. The pain of miscarrying had torn a hole in my soul; a part of me was missing, a part that I yearned for. A part I wanted back.

At the time I wondered if I'd ever feel whole again.

But I did.

In my own time.

I grieved and pushed through the pain.

And then I fell pregnant with my beautiful son and I was happier than I ever thought possible.

It twists inside. It's an ache in the belly. A heaviness in the gut; like you've swallowed a rock. And it is crippling. Then the ripples start. The ripples of uneasiness, a sense of imbalance. It spreads to the limbs which start to feel shaky. And then my chest starts to flutter as my heartbeat starts to jump around. I begin to feel breathless as the palpitations get worse. And then the panic really begins to set in. I find myself gasping for air. My body feels totally out of control, like its running away from me and I can't catch up. At this point, anxiety has taken over, and it's down to me to either drown in it or take back my power. My starting point is to focus on my breath and once I stabilise that, the rest usually follows. Sometimes this takes seconds and at other times much longer. But staying with the breathing and with the knowledge that this will pass, certainly helps me through.

Coming Full Circle

The day I finally let the words walk out of my mouth about my abuse my whole world crashed down around me. Thirteen years of silence had imprisoned me within a body that I didn't want to know, but now those words were finally free, unrestrained, understood and untamed, and little did I know that I was alchemizing my own recovery through speaking.

****

When I was eight years old I began to do everything I could to attack this temple- my body. I didn't want to recognise it, for if I saw that girl I would see her fears- they were written all over her face in a language only I could read. Anorexia grew in me like wildfire, destroying all remnants of her, and I was not afraid of those flames.

Years passed by with this illness raging within me. When I turned eighteen, I encountered another serious trauma, which sent me spiralling further down the rabbit hole. My body at this point was falling short of life. I landed in hospital, my Cheshire cat was an eating disorder that grinned at that challenge. In and out of hospital, I kept my past hidden. I couldn't say it out loud as then it would be true. If I spoke, I would be sharing the shame, the guilt, the anger, the pain, the trauma and I wanted nothing more than to forget. To wipe that slate clean, so I could carry on. But I couldn't carry on. I was falling so far down that hole that for the first time, I became afraid of the darkness and its power. I was terrified and in this fear I tried to find a reason to fight and search for the light. That reason soon came.

I was sat in a support group of eight women of different ages. We all had a serious eating disorder and we were all there to try and piece together our lives and find the light switch, so we could have that moment where it just all gets better. There, in circle, we women made our mess our message. We rose up together through connection, showing up for ourselves so that we could show up for each other, and all through two words: "me too".

For me, there are no two words in our human lexicon that are more healing than the words "me too". All of us had experience of sexual trauma and without detail, without description, we all chose to be radically vulnerable at the same time; to be raw and to surrender to the unknown.

We had been willing to connect to that "me"; to journey back to her and reaffirm that we exist, that we are not our illness, but a woman with a beating heart and wild spirit. And "too" meant we were united through our vulnerabilities and understanding, that we didn't need to say any more than *I am here with you, right now, in this group, in this space.*

Little did we know, there, in a hospital in Yorkshire on a Summer's day, we had just stepped into a sacred circle of sisterhood where we could be seen, heard and held without judgement and without apology. Through sharing in circle, we had begun to reclaim what was rightfully ours: our voice.

Later that day, I pulled my nurse aside. I told her it was time I spoke. And that afternoon, I told my story. Quietly, from beginning to end, for I had been silent for too long. From that day, I claimed back my natural feminine authority and SHE power by allowing myself to be vulnerable. I gave myself full permission to trust and to connect. It took me some years to build my life back, and I was so grateful that those walls had crashed down around me as they freed me from that prison. I learnt to tell my story loudly, unafraid and unapologetically, as this story is a part of me that has made me this person today, tomorrow, and the day after.

Now, I work with women in circle. The power of the circle remains the same, but now I do circle work to help women to return to themselves; to connect to the woman who cannot be tamed, to surrender to the full experience of healing together, in sisterhood, in a sacred, safe and welcoming space. When women come together they can move mountains. They can start to rebuild their stories and rewild their lives. And how did this all start? From those two words that say *you are not alone.*

Kate Morgan

The Lie You Sold

Hebanon snaked its way
Into the porches of my ears,
Your leperous concoction
Infiltrated my veins
Murdering the child inside
This Earth- bound flesh.
Claudius!
Your incestuous crimes
A betrayal of my Queendom;
My crown dispatched
Before coronation.
Deflowered,
I grew wild with anger
Against a betrayal I could not bear.
Truth requires thorns
And mine were sharp.
But she that dares not grasp the thorn
Should never crave the rose.
I wore my crown of thorns instead.
The thistles scratched
Unending gashes upon this skin,
Until this poison
An ante-dote was found.
Now I re-root myself
Within the ground
In soil fresh
For growing
And blooming once more.

Maria Alfieri

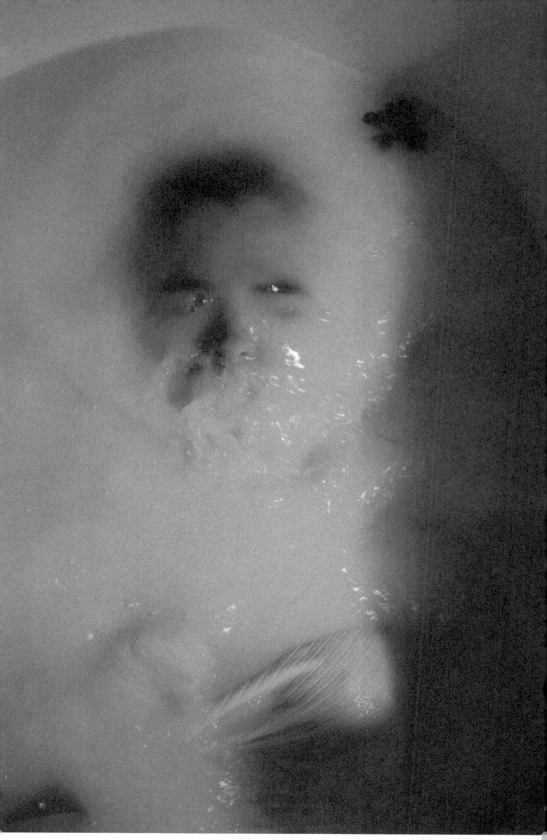

Drowning on the inside

After spending two months in hospital for my first episode of depression, I went back to work, as a nurse, on a psych ward. The local psychiatric community, being the tightly interwoven, incestuous beast that it is, afforded me no choice; it would never allow me to be silent about my time as an inpatient. Since silence was absent from the menu of options, I chose to be loud. I chose to "come out" and live openly as a mentally ill person, thinking that it would be harder for people to talk behind my back if I was already talking right out in front of them.

Except, I didn't tell people everything. I said nothing about my suicide attempts. I never told anyone that just days before I went into hospital, I'd been at work, zoning out in the middle of running the ward's community meeting, thinking instead about whether I should have KFC or something else as my final meal before suicide. *No one wants to hear that part, right?*

When my second depressive episode hit a few years later, people around me, including family, friends and co-workers, were incredibly supportive. I wasn't feeling overly suicidal, so it felt like I could tell people openly how I was feeling, and in return they were not afraid; not afraid of my illness and not afraid of me. Several people helped me out at various steps leading up to getting myself admitted to hospital. I felt like I could ask for help without being a burden on people; I felt like people helped because they wanted to help.

But as the months passed by and my depression wasn't getting better, I felt less supported, less comfortable talking to people and did feel like I was becoming a burden. My 'problem' wasn't going away, and so I became a problem to them. I took myself to hospital for the second time in less than a year and told them I was thinking about suicide, adding that I thought ECT (shock therapy) would help. Their response? To lock me in a seclusion room. They told me that I couldn't have any medication, or anything else for that matter, to help me feel more settled. I was caged in my mental and physical prison cell with nothing to distract me from the intense pain I was in. I was discharged a few weeks later feeling worse than when I had gone into hospital.

The suicidal thoughts were still there. Depression, or any mental illness for that matter, can bring out the most primitive parts of us. At a very basic level we learn from past experiences, and I had learned that asking for help meant getting locked up, and hovering in the background was the ever-present concern that my nursing career would be jeopardized. Even if I were to overcome all of that and take myself into the local emergency department, chances would be very high that I would know the mental health staff from having worked with them at some point. Um, awkward!

Since I'd learned that speaking up could cause problems, I kept my mouth shut. With the dark maelstrom of pain surging inside me, I had to grasp for any way I could to cope. The best I could come up with was to try to impose control through planning. I intended to die, and I had no desire to let anyone stop me. Planning kept me focused. I had decided that when I took action, it would need to be at the start of the three-day weekend that I had every other week. Every two weeks that day would roll around and I would be faced with a decision: to go ahead with the plan that week, or re-evaluate in two weeks. Talking to someone about it didn't even feel like an option. Eventually, decision day came around again, and I decided to move the plan into action.

Police showed up at my door three days later after I didn't show up at work. I answered the door wearing no pants; they were discarded on the floor where I had urinated. I shook like a leaf in a tornado, but somehow in my delirious mind I thought I could convince the officers that everything was okay. Even if I hadn't been totally loopy, the jig was up when they found my suicide note. Despite my delirium, I have a crystal clear memory of paramedics wheeling me out of my building on a stretcher, and as we went through the lobby I saw the woman in the building I thought of as "the crazy lady" standing there watching me. I remember thinking, *Hmm, who's crazy now?* I also remember crying, "help me, help me" over and over, as I waited in the emergency department, because my mouth was bone dry and the paramedics wouldn't give me fluids before I was seen by the ER Dr. It's strange the random things that stand out.

When I returned to work, I learned that all of those people who'd been okay with me being depressed were suddenly a whole lot less okay with me attempting suicide. Whether they were scared of my illness or scared of me is probably irrelevant, but introducing suicide into the equation had changed everything. I was unpredictable. Suddenly I had shifted from being a regular staff member to being more like a patient.

Several years have passed since my last attempt, and I'm finally starting to talk more. It doesn't always go as planned though. I was volunteering a couple years ago doing a series of talks for high school classes about suicide prevention. I decided it would make the presentations more powerful if I shared some of my own experience. It was going okay, until I encountered a class of kids that were just plain bratty. Their teacher had stepped out for a bit, leaving me to lead the class. I had talked a bit about my own history with suicide, and then moved onto some of the informational content. It was clear that the kids weren't paying attention; they were whispering to each other, on their phones, etc. I wasn't feeling particularly well to begin with around that time, but at that point I was utterly deflated. I was identifying as a suicide attempt survivor, and that didn't seem to merit even the slightest bit of respect. When the teacher returned, I said I was done and then walked out. I left a message for the volunteer agency saying those same simple words: I'm done. That was the end of that.

It wasn't my finest moment, that's for sure. It could easily have driven me back into my comfortable cave of selective silence, but I chose not to let it do that. I had fallen down, but it was time to get back up and keep talking. Clearly talking to high schoolers wasn't the right fit for me, but I could focus my efforts in other areas, and my blog turned out to be the perfect fit.

On my blog I've tried very hard to create a safe space where all mental health issues can be discussed. That meant opening up on my part, and I've been talking about suicide far more freely since starting the blog. I want to help others feel like they can talk and reach out even though I didn't. I've been able to have great conversations with others who've been through it and just get it. Through those connections I feel like I've been able to open the windows to let a little more light shine in against the backdrop of darkness that is depression.

The very act of writing, of putting my thoughts into words, is also helpful. The dialectical behavioural therapy concept of wise mind is described as the area of overlap between our rational mind and emotional mind. When my depression is bad, it's easy to settle into emotional mind and not want to budge, but writing helps me to find my way back to wise mind.

I know that it's the nature of the beast; that for me suicidality will come and go over time, sometimes triggered by stress and sometimes seemingly out of the blue. Knowing that it will go is perhaps even more important than knowing that it will come. But in some important ways things are different now. I've got strong connections to other people with mental illness that I just didn't have before; they're people that aren't scared off by talk of suicide. I've also got a doctor whom I trust, who is pragmatic and not prone to over-reacting. These changes mean that the next time things get really bad I can reach for one of these life preservers instead of drowning silently on the inside.

Ashley Peterson

Running

I've been

    Running

        All my life.

                        Running away.

Running away from pain.

My wounds.

My hurt.

I've run so   far.

    High.

And so

I've run to the point of

        collapse and exhaustion.

          I've run into the wilderness and beyond.

Until I became so

                        lost.

   And in loosing myself, I found that running was never the answer.

        To defeat the demon, you must

        Confront the demon.

So, I looked fear in the face,

      And He fell away,

           Like night gives way to the rising sun.

     And I walked all the way back home to myself.

                     Maria Alfieri

"A great photograph is one that fully expresses what one feels, in the deepest sense, about what is being photographed."

– Ansel Adams

A Self Portrait

Self-portraits have a long tradition in the art world. They've also been really misunderstood by many. Unlike what you might think, the whole point of self-portraits isn't about 'showing off', being vain, or even saying to the world: 'hey, check me out'!!! The root and motivation of doing self-photography isn't narcissism for all. Some people might do it for that reason. But I don't feel qualified, nor do I think it is right to judge the depth of the hearts of others.

For many, self-photography is part of the healing process of discovering who they truly are. It can absolutely be a part of the restoring process, helping to place together the shattered pieces of you that were broken through difficult and heart breaking experiences. Some people seem to really misunderstand the whole point of it. And that's fine. Not everyone can understand a painting, a photograph or even a song. Some people are more "matter of fact" than others. To me though, it is all about freezing a moment, capturing the thoughts, the emotions and the vibration of a soul in that moment, to be used for self-refection, to provoke and to challenge negative self-perception. There is so much we can discover about ourselves through self-photography.

Photography and I go way back. People who know me personally know how photography has always been a lifestyle and a passion, rather than just a hobby or even a job. I've always looked for the small details to remember because I soon discovered that the little things are the ones that actually make a massive difference in life. Self-portraits revealed truth to me over time and step by step, destroyed the lies that I had believed about myself for a very big part of my adult life. It is for this very reason that I have shifted the entire focus of my photography work, and now mostly work with people of all ages who have always struggled to see themselves in the beautiful way they truly are.

My most loved book is the Bible. I love the wisdom that comes from it. It inspires me, it nourishes my spirit and brings so much life to my heart. I recently read a verse that says: "Love your neighbour as you love yourself." I remember reading this many years ago realising that I wasn't able to love others wholeheartedly

because the truth was that I didn't love myself back then. I used to self-harm, speak awful words about myself and generally felt hopeless not knowing who I was anymore. Divorce almost killed me. Photography was a tool I used to reach a place of full self-acceptance. It helped me to reach a place of peace in regards to not only just my body, but also everything else that includes the woman that I was then, and the woman that I am today.

Truly loving yourself isn't expressed through vanity or thinking of yourself to be the most beautiful woman on earth. It's not about comparing and looking down on others in order to make yourself feel better. It is about learning to accept the person you are inside and outside. It is about finding God's peace, which is the only long-lasting kind. It is about being secure in the woman (or man) and person you are and knowing your worth, which is priceless.

It is about having peace in the fact that our bodies do change over the years and learning to have fun with time. It is about forgiving ourselves for the mistakes and poor choices that we made and moving forward to a better future which starts now. It is about letting go of the guilt of our failures and about celebrating the lessons that we learned along the way. It is about looking in the mirror and speaking/thinking kindness towards ourselves. It is about being truly content. It is about respecting ourselves enough to take care of our bodies and being wise in choosing healthy nourishment for body and mind.

Loving ourselves doesn't mean being vain. The meaning of beauty has been trashed and radically changed over the years. So much damage has been done. I hate the way we are lied to and told how we should look in order for us to be put in the "beautiful" basket. The world's standards are so high today that it's even hard for models to remain at that level. It's incredibly sad. But we don't have to put ourselves in that race. We will find freedom if we find the courage to let go and genuinely embrace the marvellous person we are! Both extremes – the self-hatred and the vanity – are as bad and as destructive as each other. Choose life. Choose freedom.

Flora Westbrook

sister, you are so strong

that you can be who you are

and live what

you have lived through and still,

sister, you are walking

you are smiling and you are holding

that beautiful child, who you were

forced to have, even though

he didn't actually care but sister,

we care for you, sister. we care

for you, and

for you we would do anything

because you are more than

how he defined you, or

what he made you think

about yourself and,

so you know, sister,

though your mental strength is

stronger than he ever could be

allow yourself to be vulnerable,

to us who will take you with

open arms.

-women together

sounds ring in your ears,

incessantly, though trying your best to

block. it. all. out.

and the anxiety pulsating

within my heart and the breath

losing itself, in sharp paces like

the sharp of your anger,

for now it's the sounds of your screams

and even when it's quiet

and you're not here

the screams are still there.

-*echoes*

air suffocates me

and gives me strength

at the same time.

anxiety putting me at war

not just with myself

but also, with the elements.

-*finding balance*

Gurpreet Raulia

Who am I

To dare to believe

That I can achieve

My hopes and dreams.

Who am I

To confront my fears

To be bold enough

To wipe my own tears.

Who am I

To be strong

And kind

To be connected in both body

And mind.

Who Am I

To know my own worth

To understand that sometimes,

I come first.

Who Am I

To use my voice

To let you know

That you have a choice

To be all of this and more besides.

The courage resides in

You.

Who am I?

Is a question that you need not answer;

Simply state

I am

To be your own master.

Maria Alfieri

Breaking Free

UnShamed   110

Just Me   123

Taking Shelter from the Storm   125

The Dark Art of the Heart   126

Break Away   129

Hungry Ghost   139

Caught in the Web   146

Ugliness is just a State of Mind   148

The Underlying Causes of my Eating Disorder   151

I AM   153

UnShamed

In December 2017 the Silence Breakers were named Person of the Year by Time Magazine. It was a moment that meant so much to me; I'm a Silence Breaker too. I have been speaking out about rape, and recovery from rape, for a number of years; even before my recovery, and before I set up my business ReConnected Life (which helps guide survivors to living more than one day at a time and instead living their own reconnected lives). I have known for years, before even the rape, that silence hurts; it eats us up from the inside. Speaking out is necessary to prevent the shame that silence causes, and to cast light on what lives in the shadows. Yet speaking out is a privilege dependent on what might be lost if we do: which can sometimes even be our own lives.

The #MeToo movement has been so pivotal because it did what Harvey Milk intoned gay men do in the 1970s and out themselves. He wanted to show that gays were not the very few that heterosexuals thought they were; everyone knew a gay man, they just didn't know it. Normalising the existence of homosexuals helped to bring the conversation in society to the fore. It gave momentum to the gay rights movement, and it aided understanding from the wider (heterosexual) society.

#MeToo has done the same – now everyone knows they know someone. And many people know they know more than someone. Those who felt isolated now know they are not alone. Society is starting to understand that what was in the shadows is not a rare occurrence and that rape happens to anyone of any social standing, background, sexuality, race or age. That it happens to men too. That rape and sexual assault are pandemics that need a whole rethink in how we bring up boys and make them men, and a whole rethink in how we support survivors in their recovery too (although this is still only nascent, and I am still a lone voice often). Tarana Burke began a movement which has real power and that power is causing real change.

As women we walk around with a whole host of secrets that we feel we cannot talk about and share with even our sister-friends because they are not spoken of, ever. These taboos keep us quiet, keep us in servitude to the patriarchy because society does not acknowledge the full reality of our existence. It is not just the pay gap, or the workplace innuendos, the cat-calling in the street and the holding our keys in our hand when we walk home at night. These are the things that are now starting to be talked about. But there is so much more.

Silence hurts because it builds isolation and shame. Shame, as Carl Jung said, is a soul-eating emotion. I have been thinking a lot about shame; it's something I've always proudly declared I don't feel. And yet, when I look back on my life, and specifically at the experiences that make me a woman, all I can see is shame. One layer of shame, layered upon another, again, and again. The kind of shame that is so normalised we don't even recognise it. Yet, inside, our soul is screaming.

I wonder if the lack of shame I felt about the rape was because once I had done the work to forgive myself for 'putting myself at risk' by drinking too much, the only consequence of which should be a hangover, I realised that I had not been at fault. I could not feel shame for something that had not been my fault. But my declaration that I didn't feel shame was also a way to address the deep shame I did feel and refused to acknowledge.

In order to bring into the open the layers of shame that women's lives are subjected to, I will examine how I have experienced the normalisation of shame throughout my life – and in doing so, perhaps undertake some kind of un-shaming. There is so much more than rape and sexual assault that causes us shame. #MeToo is about the violence and fear of violence that women routinely experience; in order to un-shame the feminine experience, we must also cast a light on all the other ways we as women carry shame deep in our souls.

My period first came when I was ten, five days before my eleventh birthday. I was scoring for my younger brother's cricket team, and when I went to the toilet noticed brown in my pants. My Dad said I'd become a woman now, and I squirmed. I remember feeling shame, but not knowing why. I think I was one of the first, but we didn't talk about it at school. My period was heavy, and I was always fearful of blood showing on my chair in class. I remember wearing plastic pants to catch the blood that filled the towel and the brown blood marks on knickers and clothes that would never go away.

Period shame continued through school. I remember at swim class being told it didn't matter that I couldn't wear a tampon, I could go swimming anyway. And so, I was in absolute terror that blood would get into the pool.

My breasts started showing not long after. My Mum took me to get my first bra, and I can remember the boys at school started pinging the straps and laughing. I felt like I wanted the ground to open and swallow me up.

As children we don't talk about the changes our bodies are going through. Somehow, we know it is shameful, and so we are silenced. The habit of not talking about our bodies becomes engrained as we get older, and the shame starts to become so normalised, that talking as an 'empowered' 45-year old woman to a close friend about how our periods are changing again, we both wonder, *why isn't this conversation one that happens more openly?* Why do we only know that spotting becomes normal during perimenopause when we Google it?

When I was first sexually active, I had vaginismus, which means I wasn't actually sexually active. I thought I was made wrong. When my boyfriend and I did manage to have sex, it was painful. It was only when I cheated* on him in Freshers week of university, with a boy who had a smaller appendage, that I enjoyed sex for the first time (if you're reading this; thank you). I continued to suffer from vaginismus for several years, and I couldn't wear tampons until well into my late twenties. Vaginismus was something I didn't know had a name and certainly didn't talk about with my partner (he thought I was just not that into him - which might have been the reason psychologically, although I thought I was in love). Vaginismus is rare, but not entirely uncommon; many women never speak of it even with their doctor, but it's estimated one in 500 women will experience some form of vaginismus at some point.

[*Cheating is something we also don't talk about; lots of people do it, but it is 'the' something we're 'supposed' to be ashamed of].

Not being able to wear tampons wasn't much of an issue for me because I didn't get many periods. After being very irregular they stopped almost entirely when I was with my ex-husband. Polycystic ovary syndrome (PCOS) was diagnosed. Of course, we didn't talk about it. And I didn't talk about it with any girlfriends, not really. One in ten women will suffer from PCOS at some point, but I didn't know that. I just knew I was broken somehow: my sexual reproductive organs weren't working properly. It wasn't done to speak of it and so I didn't.

Orgasms? I had my first orgasm with my ex-husband. But in that marriage, probably only one other. I remember admitting that one time to colleagues over drinks; the laughter that ensued. I decided not to share that again and would stay silent when sex became the topic of conversation. I learned how to fake it because it's easier than explaining to a man that what he's doing is nice but it's not going to happen, aware that his ego is fragile especially when it comes to sex. In all the sex I've had (and that is a lot, perhaps I should hold shame about that too, except I don't), I've only orgasmed with three men, and only two regularly. Not being able to orgasm is something not often spoken about except with humour. I think most people know this now, but I didn't then: it turns out that it's quite normal for women not to orgasm through penetrative sex. The men I was having sex with weren't trying very hard, and it really wasn't me who was malfunctioning.

When focusing the light on shame in sex, we cannot miss out masturbation, the act spoken of as natural for men, that is hidden for women. Sex and the City did a lot for my cohort of sister-girlfriends, but female masturbation is still mostly a taboo to talk about. I've been masturbating since I was about four, but I didn't know it was that. Somehow, though, I knew not to talk to about it (did my Mum discover me and tell me not to? I don't know). I don't wank like most people though. Mostly I hump. Generally speaking, I keep that to myself. I certainly don't enjoy being asked to demonstrate when a partner is laughing at me.

The first time I told anyone about my sexual fantasies, it was with my husband. We were making love at the time, close, whispering to each other; he asked my fantasy. I told him. He immediately pulled out and didn't touch me again for months, and then after that, very rarely ever again. I learned then that what

I'd feared and expected was true: masochism was dirty, disgusting, repulsive. It was years later that I discovered I wasn't the only deviant in the world, and that was mind-blowing to me. I had always dreamed that there could be clubs where you'd pay to go in, and then people would beat you. And it turns out, there are.

However, even in the world where the mantra is *Your Kink is OK*, where judgement of others' kinks is not 'tolerated', there is still fear in sharing some kinks. The girl who has been raped should not have rape fantasies, should she? Does that mean she wanted it on some level? (It doesn't). For those who don't understand, who find it abhorrent, the girl feels shame in sharing. And the girl has shared. When the girl wanks to those fantasies, it becomes shame that dominates her orgasm. Shame is complex, it takes a strong grip on the soul, digging its claws in tight.

For a long time in my life I desperately wanted children. The plan had always been, have the career, have a baby at 30 (my early adult life was not very original in its dreams and plans). Yet, pregnancy eluded me. This was of course exacerbated by the fact my husband was rarely in the mood for sex with me and seemed to have less and less sexual attraction for me as time went on. The envy I felt for the women I saw with their baby bumps was intense and unpleasant in my body. Later, after the divorce and the rape, I tried again, this time to be a single mother. This time I talked about my attempts, being public on social media about the sperm donors and the ovulation tests and the disappointment. I was covering with bluster and bravado for the deep shame I felt that my body could not do what it was designed to do. Barren. No children, and not through choice.

It's been over a decade since my marriage ended, and it's something I've mostly kept out of 'my story'. When I talk about my recovery from the rape and the PTSD, I leave out the emotional and psychological wreck I was at the time; that the fallout from the marriage mostly likely contributed to the PTSD.

My marriage had been a case study in shame. A man who felt so much shame in himself that he lashed out at any hint of criticism, creating an environment where I walked on eggshells. My ex-husband was doing what he could do with the emotional resources he had, yet those appeared to be few. And what he did was emotionally abusive.

I remember clearly, sitting on his lap, laughing, in love. I don't remember what I said, but suddenly he shoved me away with so much hatred burning in his eyes. This would be followed by days of sulking and silence. I became a shadow of myself, fearful of any comment or opinion that might set him off. He never hit me, yet I always feared it. I think perhaps if he had, maybe I would have left earlier. I did think of leaving him frequently for several years before I did and there's a big part of me that's held onto so much shame that it took me so long to make the move. Even when I share with friends now, they don't get it. No-one saw what our life was. He never hit me, so why do I call it abuse? Am I allowed to?

He stopped loving me.

I must have been terrible to live with.

It was only a bad temper.

He had his issues.

I should have helped him.

The inner dialogue is the greatest deliverer of shame, repeating the lessons learned from the outside world. And then, divorce. Why did it take me so long to leave him? *Doormat.* Why couldn't you make it work? Marriage is supposed to be forever. *Failure.* You slept with someone else. *Slut.*

After ten years of marriage, how do you make friends again?

Why did you let him isolate you in that way?

How do you even do single?

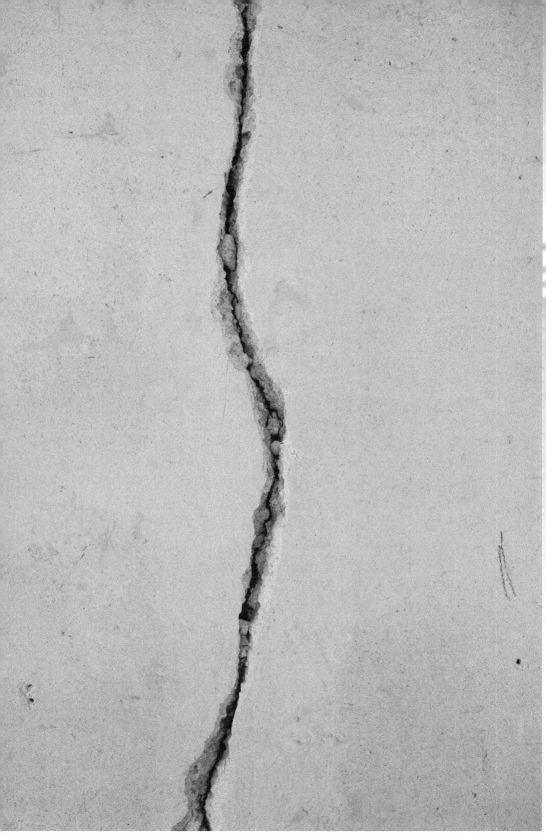

Relying on a friend to house you whilst you get yourself together.

Sleeping around, proving you can be wanted? *Slut,* again.

Taking drugs, numbing the fear that now it's all just you. *Weakling.* Cutting, to feel again. Slipping into a depression. *Shame.*

Oddly, I never felt the shame people feel for being bisexual, except I felt shame I guess for not realising that I was bisexual. I always just thought I wanted the body of the woman I fancied, or her clothes. When I realised that I wanted her, I didn't feel shame for those desires, but shame for not realising until I was thirty four years old. Maybe because I hadn't ever felt very sexual anyway, with the vaginismus, and then the acclimatising to a mostly sexless marriage for ten years. My inexperience with women though, that keeps me from making up for lost time. And I feel shame in that.

All of this was before I was raped. All of this was before I had PTSD and a mental illness and the taboo that you definitely never talk about; the shame of having let yourself get so drunk you blacked out, woke up when he was inside you, and the first thing you can say is, 'you're not wearing a condom'. The shame of not remembering clearly. The shame of not remembering what you were wearing; you're supposed to at least remember what you were wearing, aren't you? The shame of not knowing if you were drugged because you do know you were drinking a lot, but you've been drunk before, lots of times, and it's never been like that, not ever. This was the shame on top of all the other shames which were suddenly micro-shames only in comparison. This was the shame that could not, should not, ever be spoken.

Maybe because it was the shame that shouldn't be spoken, is the reason why I spoke it. I spoke it quite soon. I declared it when I returned to work. And then I learned the mistake in that. Because now I was marked as potentially unreliable, lacking resilience, and a few months later I no longer had that job. The shame went back into the box, at least for a while, until at the next job I was ignoring the shame so hard that the box exploded inside my head and I had a breakdown; they had to know.

I spoke it online continuously though. I spoke my shame and the turmoil of pain I felt inside on forums, on Twitter, hidden behind an alias, an alias some friends knew was me, but an alias that gave a veneer of distance. I became an advocate for other survivors well before I developed ReConnected Life, calling out Caitlin Moran for some misjudged comments, telling 'Luke' how wrong he was to defend Ched Evans, writing for Slutwalk, then speaking for them the next year too. Looking back, it was a natural transition when I had 'recovered' to continue to speak and advocate for other survivors in a more structured way. I do find it remarkable though that it was the big shame that I refused to be shamed by, that I spoke loudly and said 'you might judge but this is me', and yet the micro shames that came before, feel more shameful. The way I rationalise it is that all the times before when I did not speak of the shame I felt, and instead let it fester in me, those little shames grew inside, so that when the rape came there was no room left for shame. It was like it exploded and left me with the scars inside. The screams inside could not be silenced anymore.

There have been other shames in my life too. I was unemployed for a long period after I lost the job for being unreliable. Standing in line at the job centre is not an experience I'd recommend to anyone. As a business owner I've been between contracts several times too, and that feels shameful; not yet having a thriving successful business that's paying its own way. Having debt and still over-spending all the time; taking comfort from buying things. These things are shameful. But they are the shame of any human. Most of us are one pay-cheque away from destitution; it's only the very lucky ones who can save to have that six month buffer that is recommended. And yet there is still the shame in not having it. The shame of having had the house and now renting at forty five, knowing that the housing ladder is increasingly out of your grasp due to both rising prices and your age. Twenty years to pay off a mortgage is fast disappearing as an option.

It's the shames that are specific to the lived experience of (cis) women that I have exposed through sharing my shames. There are other shames that many women also experience that we don't talk about, that I haven't experienced. Abortion. Miscarriage. Being childless by choice. And the new shames I'm experiencing through perimenopause, and the many more shames I'm sure are yet to come. And of course those that I don't even know about to mention – because they are hidden, unspoken and shameful.

As a gender shame is engrained. Men have their shames too, and of course I'm not suggesting that they don't. The shame that is engrained in us as women from the time we start menstruating and getting breasts is so constant; it becomes an insidious worm, destroying the joy of the feminine so that instead of stepping into our divine, feminine, soft power, we are made small by it. How can we as women step into our power, when we are made ashamed of everything that makes us women?

We are shamed by our femininity. We hide it even whilst we vamp ourselves up and put on the clothes and make-up and wear our masks. Authenticity, realness; these are virtues that are being extolled in an age where you can't tell real news from fake. But how real are we when we can't say out loud, *I'm having a head-sweat day, these hot flushes are the worst,* for fear of being seen as weak? How real are we when we can't say *actually the Endometriosis is killing me, it's a chocolate and duvet day, I'll be far better when this period is done with?* How real are we when we quietly pretend everything is fine, when inside we're dying because our period came and we're not pregnant, again?

Speaking up and speaking out is a privilege. And yet the more of us who do it, the more normalised it will become. The more we are willing to un-shame ourselves, the more of us can live unashamed. Our un-shaming will make unashamed the norm, so that others can step out of shame as well. When we can un-shame all the micro shames and step into our feminine power, the patriarchal grip will release, and a profound paradigm shift will have occurred. Imagine a world where women are free from shame. Imagine how powerful we will be then. Imagine.

Emily Jacob

Just Me

After years spent trying to unravel the cause of my pain, identify the triggers of my emotional instability and volatility, the reasons for my numbness and feelings of isolation, I awoke one morning to the realisation that I didn't have that drive to self-destruct anymore.

It

had

just

gone.

You see, I'd been on this journey of self -discovery for quite some time.

I'd read thousands of books, been to counselling, watched vlogs, signed up to various online courses and webinars.

I'd changed my wardrobe, my style, my hair.

I changed my diet, my fitness routine, my friends.

I stopped allowing toxic people into my life.

And although to some extent my life had improved, I still felt empty.

Dissatisfied.

No amount of money, clothes, food or working out was going to fill that void anymore.

What was missing, was **me.**

Not the should-me, or the thin-me, the rich-me, the academic-me, the fit-me, the stylish-me or the could-be-me but

just

ME.

I'd been shutting **me** out.

Worried that **just -me** wasn't enough.

I'd gone through life acquiring badges, certificates, medals and awards to prove myself worthy. I'd put just-me aside to accommodate the needs of everyone else first.

And then wondered why I felt resentful and angry.

No matter what I did, I was never **good enough.**

Until I realised that **I** was to blame for my own not-enoughness.

So, I started to show myself compassion and self-care. I made time for just-me. I allowed myself to rest when I needed, to nourish myself properly, to spend time in nature, to put my own needs first. I learned to say no. I stopped worrying about the future. I left the past **behind.**

And then I woke that glorious morning, with a serene sense of peace and the realisation that

Just-me

is enough.

MS

Taking Shelter from The Storm

"I sat in my car with my head in my hands, not knowing if I'd ever go back. I was so overwhelmed by my darkness, I just wanted to run away, to escape. But there is no escaping the darkness until you confront it head on- that black hole will just follow you around everywhere, sucking the life out of you. So, I decided to reach out. To tell someone about my deeply negative thoughts, not necessarily because I thought it would end them, but because I hoped it would ease the weight of their burden. And it did.

Now, when I feel that storm coming, I take shelter from it with others, rather than enduring its power on my own. To some extent, its true what they say- a problem shared is a problem halved; mainly because sometimes our own negativity creates worst case scenario's in our head, which when spoken out loud, lose some of their impact."

The Dark Art of the Heart
The Hidden Healing Power of Heartbreak

As soon as we met, a spark took hold of my soul. It burnt long and slow for you. Finally, I submitted, and almost instantly my inner world was engulfed with fierce flames. I literally melted, and part of me forever fused to you, opening up a channel of energy between us. It buried deep into my very core, taking root.

But then you pulled away so fast you ripped my very self out from me, pulling and heaving until you wrenched out the deep repressed shadow parts of me.

I chased you in panic at the sudden separation, and ran right into it; all of my dark despair, my demons deeply buried - now all-encompassing and overwhelming. I had to start to shine some light on them, as I was now surrounded with nothing but the scarred and barren chambers of my heart. From the dying embers of that same fire, I revived my essence to light the shadows I had avoided. Then you were drawn back by the distant flicker of sparkle, snapping right back to me as though you'd been on a tensed elastic.

Reunited with you once more, my core felt complete. The emptiness was gone, but soon it was clear- it was only the remainder of my demons left swirling in the space where my soul used to be, forced abruptly back inside when the gap closed between us.

Then you tore off again, and brought them back through the surface once more. I stood opposite my shadow self in all its horror, and felt ashamed at the fearful, selfish and insecure aspects of myself. The deep depression and grief I ignored. I could have turned and looked away. I could have run in another direction, and then kept on running. I could have stepped into the shadows and re-absorbed them, forcing them further down into the recesses of my being, but I didn't.

I started to run for you again, but I was completely lost in the darkness. The last of the embers turned to ash, and I had no light left to shine. This time I stopped and stood still to face those shadows. I was tired of running. I had to set myself free and completely dig you out at the root. I knew I would be left with emotional burns and permanent scars, but these I would bear proudly as a mark of the sincerity of feeling and signs of healing. In a way I felt lucky, as a heart never broken open is a heart with no scope to look inside and expand.

****

So what do I do now- just my shadow-self and I? I am hollow inside- if I absorb the shadows I will become them. So, I must take them by the hand and walk beside them; no ignoring or running. This is how to truly love oneself and others; to accept and love the parts we deem 'ugly' and 'unworthy'. Love will allow security for the shadow to stay in step. The shadow parts of ourselves must not be shamed or denied. Being so exposed and open to my darkness also brings the blessing of love and light from other sources. I find that friends and soul team- mates allow me to absorb their light, like one candle lighting another. And so I begin to burn brighter again, enriched by the luminous energy I had once been so blind to. Thank You.

****

This piece is written about the depression I experienced after the break-up of a toxic relationship, but the breaking point forced me to look inwards and to revaluate my expectations of, and attachments to relationships, including the relationship I have with myself. I can only speak from my own experience; there are as many heart-breaks as there are hearts and everyone's experience, feelings and timeline are their own, and all are equally valid. Personally, I have learnt there is always love and light around me, and it took a journey into the deep dark for me to be able to recognise this. I hope by sharing this I can ignite a spark of recognition in someone in a dark place too.

Cheryle Brown

Break away

from everything you thought you should do and find your true happiness

Do you ever hear certain words or phrases coming out of your mouth and think, *Hang on, those aren't my words, I don't actually think that?!* Most of the time we just brush over it and move on with our day, but when you start becoming more aware of your words, it can stop you in your tracks. Then the questions start:

Whose words were they?

Where has this come from?

What do I actually think/feel/want?

This, I have learnt, is one of the key aspects to breaking free from what you "should" do and starting to fill your life with only the things that you really want.

Let me explain how I came to this conclusion.

Firstly, let me be clear; I had one of the most privileged upbringings, both financially and emotionally. I have a loving and supportive family. We will all do anything for each other. We are tight, and for the most part I would actually choose my family as friends. We never wanted for anything growing up and I am truly grateful for that. That being said, it's important to understand that having this kind of upbringing does not protect you from what I would call societal "shoulds".

As you navigate your way through life, going to school, interacting with other humans, engaging in media of all kinds and eventually getting a job, you encounter an array of (often subtle) feedbacks that help shape your perception of yourself and your goals in life. These experiences develop your idea of your place in the world and will also create an idea of all the things you "should" do in your life.

Let me give you an example. Despite having a family who did not treat me differently because I am a girl and, if anything, encouraged me to do anything I wanted no matter what, I spent most of my youth wishing I was one of the boys. Purely and simply because life seemed much easier and more fun for men.

As I grew up, I noticed the boys got to do more fun stuff at school like play football or rugby and we got netball and hockey (which I hated). This belief was reinforced throughout my life. As I started studying Law at University, I observed that most of the successful solicitors and barristers were men and actively only socialised and networked with each other (a crucial part of managing clients).

In my first office job I experienced having my voice dismissed in meetings in a team full of male managers, and even lost a quality candidate because "he needed a strong fatherly figure not a pretty little girl manager". Brutal right?

Even my social life wasn't untouched by this. I watched the stag parties go off and play go karting and paintball, whilst I got to join in on hen parties that always seemed to focus on getting ourselves looking really pretty and then sitting nicely drinking cocktails or tea.

Everywhere I looked I found evidence of how men and women did different things and were meant to act in different ways and that was just how it was. I forever felt like I didn't quite fit in anywhere.

It is fair to say that I did what I think most women who end up in male dominated work environments do; I embodied the distorted masculine qualities that would ensure my success in a male dominated world. I defied everything I had learnt that a woman "should" do and how a women "should" act. I was strong, outspoken and learnt to completely shut down my emotions, to the point that I was commended as being the least emotional manager, like this was a good thing!

I knew in order to succeed I would not be able to have a family, as this was a reason I would not get a promotion. In fact, I remember hearing this as valid interview decision making criteria. A female candidate had just gotten married, so it was agreed that she would probably get pregnant soon and was therefore not a wise hire.

I was vocal about my decision to not have a family and that my focus was on my career, to ensure of my constant success and promotions. I accepted that I couldn't have it all; I had to choose and I chose my career. I chose what I considered to be success; more money, more status, my own property, nice holidays and a lovely stash of money for a rainy day.

What I didn't realise was I had just replaced one "should" with another. I was doing everything you "should" do to be happy, as defined by society, not me. I had jumped from the frying pan straight into the fire and I was totally oblivious.

The problem with "shoulds" is that if they are not in-line with what you actually want, then eventually they will fall apart and it's rarely very pretty, especially if your whole life is built on them.

The unravelling of me living in the "shoulds" started when I was twenty seven.

After a break up with my partner of seven years, I found myself living alone with no daily emotional support to help me manage my incredibly stressful job. The anxiety that I had unknowingly carried my whole life started to take over. It was a very quick downward spiral of panic attacks, a new and very volatile relationship, not to mention falling back into dabbling with drink and drugs.

Looking back it is so clear that this was a pattern repeating throughout my life, having done something very similar aged nineteen.

This time around though it was so much more intense. I was hell bent on keeping it together at work and that meant a constant repression of my emotions. Unfortunately, those emotions we so often push down don't go away and one day they all came out. Years of denying my feelings and holding it together came out and I plummeted into depression. Weirdly, it was a welcome respite after the height of the anxiety for months. My body crashed hard.

The moment I realised it was really bad was a day I will never forget. I was at my parents' house with my nephew. Now, anyone who knows me knows that my nephew is my world - I have never felt love like that! But this day I distinctly remember playing with him and him hugging me, but I couldn't feel anything. I mean, I knew I still loved him, but I couldn't feel it. I felt numb. The tears just kept falling but I didn't even feel sad.

I was stood in my parent's utility room looking into the fridge, tears streaming down my face, and my dad came over to me and said, "Katie, this isn't you. Something is wrong, you need to talk to someone." That was the moment I knew. He was right. I needed help big time. This wasn't something I could do alone because I had no idea how.

I wish I could say that was the turning point but it wasn't, it got worse. I was taking steps to understand how to work through this. I was signed off work, I started slowing down, seeing a therapist and getting out in nature. I started sessions in floatation tanks, but really I was desperately hoping someone would just fix it for me.

On my twenty eighth birthday, I found out a childhood friend of mine took his own life and it shook my world hard. In that moment that I heard the news, I understood it. I want to be really clear, I have never considered taking my own life; I was lucky that it never got that bad for me. But, I also know that people who take their own life do not want to die, they just want it to stop. Whatever their battle is; anxiety, depression, addiction, they just want it to stop, and I understood that feeling. It completely terrified me.

There were times I got so scared, that I would call my mum in tears, because I just couldn't stop crying and I would get panic attacks from the completely overwhelming feelings. I lived about a forty minute drive from my parents and my mum would send my dad to pick me up and I would stay at their house. I used to call them "rescue missions" and that's pretty much what they were to me. I was scared to be alone.

The Turning Point

It was one of these "rescue mission" nights, a Saturday. I was in a complete state, pacing around my flat, panicking. I called my mum. She told me they were out and had been drinking so they weren't able to drive to pick me up. I had a few choices; get a taxi, call a friend or try to deal with this myself.

I found somewhere in between...Google! I Googled how to help depression for probably the millionth time and I saw yoga. I remembered that I did yoga when my anxiety was bad before and it worked. Maybe, just maybe, it could help.

It was worth a try. So I found a video by Esther Ekhart called *Yoga for Depression*, got on my mat and cried my way through the class. By the end of it, the uncontrollable sobs were easing and I felt calmer. I was able to get into bed and sleep.

That was the turning point. From there I gradually built up the ability to help myself and rebuild my life. Yoga was the solid foundation for that. I built in regular classes to my week, both online classes at Ekhart Yoga and group classes in a studio round the corner from my flat. I even started Yoga Teacher Training with the sole aim to go deeper into my practice and understand why it helped me so much. I had no intention of teaching yoga at the time, I just wanted to know more.

Yoga started to change my life, but this was only the beginning. Many people think of yoga as something purely physical, but there is so much more to it. One of the best things I uncovered throughout my journey with yoga was the crucial need for self- enquiry.

Self -enquiry is what helps you move away from living in the world of "shoulds" and into a place of acting from your true desires, needs and wants. I believe this to be one of the keys to lasting happiness. It doesn't happen overnight and it is a constant practice to stay connected to what you really desire, but it is so worth the effort.

These are the steps that I still live by now and I can honestly tell you they have transformed my life:

Start a morning routine

Make time for yourself. Even just ten minutes can transform your day. It is so easy for us to just jump out of bed and get straight into all the things that need to be done right now, but that puts us into a heightened state. Take some time to slow down and ease into your day. What you do in that time can be personal to you. I tend to do the steps below, as it sets up my day so nicely and allows me to connect to what I really want and not just do what needs to be done.

Meditate

Meditation doesn't need to be fancy. Just ten deep belly breaths is a pretty good start and you can do it anywhere. I used to do it on the loo at my high stress office job and it became a habit every time I was in there. I just made the most of the time I had as I was always "too busy" to meditate. When I noticed my breath becoming shallow and had crept up into my chest, which would just be increasing the fight or flight response in my body, I knew I had to bring my breath back into my belly. Just ten breaths would be enough to bring me back to a grounded centre, ready to carry on my day. This slowing down is the foundation for self- enquiry, as when you are spinning around with a million thoughts in your head, it is impossible to make sense of it all.

Yoga

Sometimes you need a little more assistance to slow things down and this is where yoga really shows off. Breathing consciously into your belly whilst moving the body calms the nervous system and also distracts you from a busy mind. Eventually you create enough space in the mind and body to sit still in meditation.

There are so many different types, teachers and ways to do yoga. From online classes, to studios, workshops and retreats. I personally love all of them, but I recommend trying a few different ways before you rule out yoga as "not for you".

Journal

Journalling is where I get the most insight into whether I am acting from a "should" or from a place of what I truly want. It is less about what I did that day and more about how I am feeling and what is in my head. It is amazing the clarity you get by writing. It is like you are able to step back and clearly observe what is going on. It creates space between you and the overwhelming thoughts. You'll eventually notice patterns of things you write about, which are clues to the "shoulds" and real wants in your life.

Gratitude

Another thing that gives you clues as to what fills you with joy and means you are acting from what you really desire rather than what you "should" be doing. It is also a great way to start your day positively and switch up your perspective on your life. This is so important in times of change and transformation, as it does get bumpy moving from living a life of "shoulds" and into a life of everything you actually choose.

This morning routine for me keeps me checked in with myself and is quite a personal process of self- enquiry.

It is possible to have assistance with self- enquiry though. I am very grateful to have worked with a few different therapists and coaches that have hugely assisted me in my journey into understanding what I truly desired.

Share your thoughts

Vocalising things can be an incredible way to work out what you actually want. I am amazed at the amount of times I have said things aloud just to follow up with "erm....actually, that's not true" and with a trusted and experienced teacher or therapist they can gently assist you into uncovering the truth. The reason I opt for a professional and not a friend is that they won't tell you what to do, or think, or tell you what they think. Instead they ask questions, or just hold space for you to work things out yourself. Although I am aware that not all professionals do this, so just be mindful of who you work with. Look for people who can hold space for you to work things out yourself without telling you answers. Let's be honest, if you aren't certain what you want, how on earth could someone else tell you?! It is called self- enquiry for a reason.

Keep checking in

If you pick up a morning routine like this you should stay relatively connected to your truth and act daily from a place that will bring you lasting happiness, but do remember to check in with the bigger picture now and again. Look at your life overall and just challenge yourself on whether this is actually your decision or another one of those pesky "shoulds" that you picked up along the way.

****

Note on the concept of "distorted masculine"

I want to make a really important point here. I call these behaviours "distorted masculine" as there is a huge distortion in what is considered a masculine quality. The whole concept of "boys don't cry" and "manning up" is complete nonsense. Everyone, regardless of gender, needs to be able to freely express their emotions, both good and bad. Ironically, as I have done more work around this I actually no longer believe that life is easier or better as a man. Both men and women have challenges, neither of which are easier or better than the other. I can officially say that I am very happy to be a woman now and no longer think it would have been easier if I was a man!

Katie Finch

Hungry Ghost

London. 2009.

I feel my depression like a heavy coat. It's soaked with negative self- talk. I spend my life in the shadows, somewhere between the veil of the unknown and the conscious. My nerves are gnawed and my mind broken, hounded by self-obsessive thoughts which perpetuate the hollow landscape trapping me in the dark place in which I find myself.

As I walk the lonely city streets, I feel I am disappearing atom by atom, no one notices. Other days I am fragmenting; sharp prisms of the glass walls I hide behind sliver away leaving me exposed and terrified. But still no one notices.

In Chinese Buddhism, it is believed that we move through six realms on the Wheel of Life. These realms represent all of human existence. In the lower realms reside the Hungry Ghosts. They are depicted as creatures with huge bellies that are perpetually empty, they have pinhole mouths and tiny necks – they are unconscious beings with no awareness of their deep hunger, they don't know how to feed themselves and so the cycle continues. In Sanskrit, Hungry Ghosts are called 'departed one' - I was the 'departed one' – pursuing something outside of myself with an insatiable thirst but no awareness of what 'it' was.

****

Looking back I see that I was deeply unhappy in a career and a world that wasn't nourishing my soul. I was starving but I didn't know what to eat. I ate what I knew, swallowed it down whole and worse became constipated with angst, pain and total lost-ness. I didn't know what I didn't know. I knew something was wrong but it wasn't tangible...reachable... touchable....like a spark of light that moved when you tried to focus on it...elusive, a spectre.

I knew something was very wrong but the fear of accepting this, sharing it or even finding a compassionate way to hold my self was a million miles from where I was. Years of 'doing' kept the dysfunction of my childhood tucked away; alcoholism, anger issues, uncomfortable sexual interest from an adult man I trusted.

I left home very young and travelled. I ignored the niggles and the triggers, going from one relationship to the next. I struggled with emotional intimacy; a cold fish. I buried it all for years because life calls. And so I'd put on my mask, I'd smile, I'd engage, show interest, laugh. But it was a lie. I was dying inside. I was told I had it all; good looks, health, a career, a quick wit, intelligence. I was an attractive, eligible female. But this only triggered further guilt and shame: *I did have it all- didn't I?*

I searched book shops for meaning, scanning the shelves for something, anything. What was the elusive spot? I spent years in a cycle of pretence, feeling like an impostor.... I was a liar, a fraud and I was cheating life.

The Universe provides

I spiralled to a place so low that there was nowhere else to go. I stood on Chelsea Bridge imagining jumping. My pain was too big. Gigantic. Some people think that it is a selfish act. To kill yourself. I believe that in this hopeless place it feels like the only option. The shame and guilt reinforce the thought and it starts to embed. It seems like the most natural final act and my skewed thinking romanticised it.

I fantasised about how it would be. It gave me comfort. And then I would come full circle into a place of self- loathing. I was self-obsessed and couldn't see beyond my own feelings, and so I remained stuck in a perpetual cycle of negative thoughts. In retrospect I think I had to be pushed to the edge of despair so that I could find myself again. I had to be so sick and tired of being sick and tired, so that I could find a crack to let the light in enough to allow awareness to grow around my shockingly poor self-care.

I was entrenched in a culture of work that celebrated over working, always giving 110% of yourself. Start early. Work late. Go hard or go home.

"She is fully committed."

"Always carries things through."

"Fun party girl."

These comments led me to continually neglect my own self- care. I attended every work meal and night out, drinking copious amounts of wine that numbed the moment. I spent so many nights out with people who didn't care about me, just who I was in the company and what career steps I could help them with. I hammered the gym to hone and tone my body and wear designer labels. I layered mask after mask, using them interchangeably throughout my long, stressful days to become what I believed was expected of me.

It took years for me to understand my patterns of behaviour around over working and poor self –nurturing. I thought because I was a vegetarian, exercised and drank water that I had good self –care! But I hadn't paid attention to or honoured my spiritual self-care. My lack of self- love meant that I was so hard on myself. I believed on some level that I was un-loveable; love and healthy sex were for other people. Hard work and pushing myself to the edge in everything was my mantra.

I left London exhausted, disconnected and lonely. I used to read books. I always felt a connection with them; they give and invite. I could be a voyeur to the narrative. But for some reason I had stopped reading.

In 2010 I was in Totnes, Devon walking around a wonderful book shop. I realised just how much I missed reading. I was still low but seeking answers. I scanned the shelves; mindfulness, religion, esoterical. I picked up a book called *Dark Nights of the Soul* by Thomas Moore. I picked it up, read the back, put it back and continued looking. The window rattled and I noticed that the book had fallen from the shelf. I thought the wind blowing through the window must have blown it off. I put it back, left the shop, and had a coffee.

But I couldn't get the book out of my mind. *Was this a message from the universe? Synchronicity?* I went back and ran my hand along the window. There was no cold air, no breeze.

I bought the book.

And on reading it cover to cover, something clicked. This was a rite of passage, a transitional phase. Thomas Moore quotes in Part Two:

' A man must wrestle till the dark centre, that is shut up close, break open, and the spark lying therein kindle.' - Jacob Boehme (On True Resignation).

This dark night was a gift, an un-trodden pathway full of infinite potential. There is beauty in this place; a breaking down of old to make way for the new. The spark within was there but it still wasn't enough to allow it to fill me up.

I believe my soul was whispering to me for years, but I didn't listen. When the whispers became louder, I still didn't listen. I couldn't hear them; no one teaches you how to listen to the whispers of your soul. It wasn't until those whispers became a shout that I had no choice but to acknowledge them. The universe literally shunted me that day in that book store from a place of fear, isolation and unhealthy practices, to a place in-between.

It's difficult to describe, but it felt bigger than me; a source of power and connection outside of myself whilst connecting deeply to my innate knowing of what was good for me. It takes strength, determination and courage to leave a familiar and safe place and to meander into the realms of self- discovery. I understand that I have created mental constructs that give foundation to my perception of reality. I took these as absolute truths.

The shunt into a new direction wasn't easy. I was riddled with self- doubt. I had to be gentle and kind with myself and take one day at a time. I walked in nature, daydreaming whilst walking my sister's dog. I allowed myself space. It took a while to accept that I didn't need to be going all of the time. The more I relaxed, the more I let go. Surrender is a word that I read in books. I didn't feel safe enough to surrender, but I felt safe enough to relax and gently let go, sometimes pulling up the reigns when I was afraid, or when the old patterns came knocking on my door. With practice I learnt to trust my intuition, to listen to my body and open my heart to the potential of what may come for me.

I feel that I am more in tune, able to take or leave what doesn't serve me and to be whole hearted and more open with people. My sense is that as we let go and simplify our lives the more expansive we become. My inner landscape flourished as my external life grew. There is more colour, magic, love and a feeling of contentment. I surround myself with my own tribe; people that resonate with my understanding of life. I've learnt that happiness is not static; contentment flows within me and at times I feel great joy.

There was no definitive moment for my depression, more a collective building of experiences over many years, each loss opened up other losses and the sum became greater than the whole.

I am grateful for my own *Dark Night of the Soul*. It taught me to explore within and gave my life shade and texture. It introduced me to my Hungry Ghost, which shone a light into the areas of spiritual longing and awakened my hunger for spiritual connection.

Making little changes in my life helped. More time in nature, walking, healthy food, a commitment to work on myself and to honour what I do well. I am tender with myself as I peel the layers of old thought patterns and beliefs, challenging them and letting go of that which was holding me back. Some of this work I have done alone and some through education, retraining to be a counsellor, sitting in circle with like- minded women who love and honour the feminine/ masculine aspects of their identity.

Small steps lead to bigger outcomes. My first step was to *allow* spaciousness within, so that my innate self could find its path. It is now ten years since I first wrote about my depression. If I have a bad day I go back to my self- care strategy. It's normally because I am doing too much, not saying no and taking on too much. It isn't selfish. It is self- care. We can't be of service to others unless we are emotionally integrated ourselves. We will always have challenges, parts will fragment and drop away, new aspects will grow and reintegrate. Building emotional resilience is the foundation for my own growth and development. I believe that developing awareness allows us choice and choices bring about change.

Trudi

Caught in the Web

Caught in a web
Of sticky lies.
The silken thread,
Delicate.
Disguising
Its strength
To consume and contain
It's prey.
You're drawn to its beauty,
Walking into the spin,
But you cannot escape
Now that you're in.
The candyfloss texture
Once saccharine
Now exposed;
The sweet life you were chasing
Tastes good at first,
But you're left with an
Inquenchable thirst.
You're trapped
In the web that's been weaved.
Regret.
Shame.
Anxiety.
All rising.
In panic

You twist and turn
In your bonds.
Your heart,
A drum
Banging
Out of Rhythm.
Slow Down.
Breathe.
Patience.
The emotional storm will pass.
And in the calm,
The key
You'll find
To unlocking your mind.
And a way out
You will find.
Freedom is
Understanding
Ourselves
And the world we inhabit.
Recognise
Mistakes
And wrong turns
As tools for growth.
Find gratitude
For the web into which you walked;

It ultimately saved you.

Maria Alfieri

"*I spent my entire life feeling ugly...*"

...until one day I realised that ugliness is just a state of mind.

The underlying causes of
my eating disorder

It took me years to discover

that my eating disorder was a manifestation

of my depression and anxiety.

The eating disorder was the 'drug'

I used to escape the

depression and relieve the anxiety.

But those eating behaviours

only really fed into the

depression and anxiety.

Once I recognised this cycle,

and untangled all the separate parts,

it became so much easier to tackle.

I AM....

A woman, a teacher, an ethicist, philosopher, friend, only child, orphan....This is not a story of despair, but one of hope, from someone who has struggled.

I had a very happy childhood. I was loved by my parents and when I was fifteen and my Dad died, my Mom loved me for the two of them. School was OK. I was never really a part of what you would call the 'in crowd', I was chubby, not very sporty and quietly studious. I was incredibly shy, especially with other children and would literally hide behind my Mom when anyone spoke to me. God knows how I made it to be narrator in every school play!

I got into University, the one I wanted in London to study the subjects I was most interested in – Philosophy and Theology. I made friends, some of whom are still good friends and after graduating I went on to do a PGCE to become a teacher, something I had always wanted to do. Less than six weeks in I realised I wasn't ready for it; how do you teach an eighteen year old when you are only twenty one? I worked for two years in London doing a series of jobs that everyone told me I was over qualified for, and finally went back and did my PGCE.

There are two real stand out things in this chapter of my life, which maybe now wouldn't go unnoticed if I'd ever mentioned it, which I didn't; admission is a sign of weakness isn't it and I wasn't weak...*was I?*

Firstly, my Dad used to work shifts and as a child I could never rest until he was home from his night and afternoon shifts. I think I was always an anxious child; I don't know why as I was loved and secure. I used to like everything in its place and ordered, which included my Dad being home from work when he was supposed to be.

I remember the day in early July when he and Mom had been to an appointment at the hospital. He'd knocked his finger at work (he worked in a rubber factory) a few weeks earlier and had developed a cough. I'd never known my Dad to be ill. He was strong- he'd survived Malaria in WWII for God's sake. I came home from school and no-one really said much, but we all knew he wasn't well, and he never went back to work. His cancer diagnosis did not come until three weeks before he died on the 27th September 1977. My Mom and I watched him diminish before our eyes for nearly three months, until they took him into hospital three days before he died.

My Dad was over six foot tall and strong. When he got ill, he stopped eating, his energy decreased and he would lie on the floor in a foetal position trying to get rid of the pain. I will never forget that image. He would sometimes eat a chocolate bar. I made Damson jam. He said it was lovely.

I couldn't help him. All I wanted to do was get away. I loved him so much and I couldn't solve it, I couldn't make it better. It made me angry. I was used to solving problems and I could do nothing.

I was angry.

I am still angry.

The night he died, I went to see him in the evening. He was completely lucid. His vision however, which had been poor, was fine and he was combing his hair. He asked me why I looked so sad, but I couldn't answer. He told me he loved me and I told him I loved him too. He said everything would be fine. Mom and I left at 10.30pm. He died at 10.45pm. It was not fine.

I went to school the next day and was removed from the form room whilst my classmates were told. It wasn't mentioned again. I didn't cry in front of my Mom, nor she in front of me. We had to be strong. It wasn't until years later that we both admitted to this.

I miss my Dad. He'd been through so much in the war, from being forced to fight for the Germans, escaping, joining the Partisans, fighting with the allied forces in the UK and never returning to Poland to see his family. Cancer got him at fifty five and that was that. Forty one years later I am still angry that I was powerless to do anything. I miss him like mad. He never saw anything I achieved in my life; he gave me my love of Philosophy and now he is not here to share it with.

When he died, my Mom and I used to go to bed and I remember waking in the night and having to go and check that she was still breathing. I still do this with my partner now.

The second thing that stands out, as I recall, was when I was doing my teaching practice in South West London. I remember getting on the bus and suddenly shaking uncontrollably. I felt sick- just nerves I thought- but it didn't go away. I completed my PGCE and existed on dry toast and baked potatoes, as the sick and shaky feeling continued.

Very few people knew that every day I would shake at the thought of being in a classroom. I always had to be there first at the door to greet my students and have a chat to make them feel welcome. Then came the challenge of making a subject perceived as 'boring' come to life; there was never a waking minute in my thirty-ish years of teaching where I was not looking for something new or innovative or exciting. I was never still in a classroom; not because I had so much energy- I am lazy by nature- but because if I stood still I would shake too much. I would analyse every lesson and worry that I had missed something. I would mentally beat myself up if someone told me they had done something a certain way- *why didn't I think of that?*

In my first two jobs in teaching I used to avoid the Staff Room; I hated the gossip and the small talk and used to sit marking in a quiet space. I am still amazed that I am in touch with people from those schools.

I became Head of Department when I was twenty eight, not a bad achievement for someone who had little self-belief. I taught abroad between 2001-2009 and 2016-2017 at an international school, but now I do very little teaching and I do miss it.

I took a break from teaching in 2009 because I thought I was becoming stale. I went and did a Drama course, focused on directing, and was fortunate enough to work for periods of time with the late Sir Peter Hall, Dame Judi Dench and did a stint as assistant director on a new play at The Royal Court Theatre in London. I also did a cookery course and met some great chefs. An interesting interlude, but I felt I could hack neither; there was always someone better than me, so I returned to teaching.

My Mom died in 2012 and I became a real-life orphan Annie. Her death knocked me and I was left in a constant state of *what more could I have done?* Did I do enough? Should I have recognised the signs of her being so unwell?

My Mom had always been a brick and the way she coped after my Dad died was amazing. She took her first flight with me to France when she was sixty and continued to travel to see me well into her seventies. She was slowing down in the last year of her life, but her mind was as sharp as ever. I saw her at the very end of July 2012. She was fine, if a little slow, but three weeks later, she was dead. I was with her and held her hand as she slipped away. Again, I couldn't stop it.

I had experienced something similar many years before, when a student in my tutor group committed suicide just days before her eighteenth birthday. I can picture her now, sitting crossed legged on a desk in our form room talking about how she wanted to be famous, to be remembered. She made it; her suicide was a double one. She and her friend made the national press. I had to tell my tutor group, her friends, of that devastating loss on that Monday morning. Even today I wonder how I missed those signs. *Where was I to not really understand what she was saying?*

My mind still goes over all of these things. It never rests. I see that in so many areas where I think I have failed. I berate myself for my lack of determination, at my inability to persevere, at my laziness.

All the deaths I have encountered of those close to me, including former students, have left me with a gap and the question...If only?

If only:

- I'd recognised the signs…Liz's desperation, my Mom and Dad's declining health.

- I'd been there more.

- I could have changed it (which I probably couldn't).

Whilst working at a school in the Netherlands, the moment of a meltdown finally arrived in early October 2017. I got ready for work one morning and then could not get through the front door, no matter how hard I tried and how hard I spoke to myself. Diagnosis: total burn out. Advice: if you can afford it, take a break and look after yourself. Fortunately, I could.

I am trying to look after myself, but it is not easy as I still have a voice in my head that says *you failed*.

Overwhelmingly the feelings are:

- Sadness, at the gaps that have been left in my life. I know people cannot live forever, nor would I ever want people to suffer unnecessarily.

- Guilt, because I should have done better, I should have recognised the signs.

- Anger, which is still all-consuming, and rises like bile in my throat. The anger is directed at me because I don't think I am a very nice person; I know that I am selfish and if I could be more selfless, then who knows….

I like to feel in control. Death means that I am not. Logically, I know I cannot change things. Emotionally, I am still very angry. The angrier I get, the more guilt I feel and the more self-destructive I become. It's a vicious circle.

There are still lots of things going on in my head which will take time for me to understand and work through, but it will work out. I did a Masters degree in Ethics at Utrecht University where my Professor asked, "Why do you always say 'I am JUST a teacher.'"

That sticks with me...

On reflection I am more than *just* a teacher. The 'just' I'm sure, plays down the importance of my role as a teacher and certainly demonstrates a lack of worthiness, which I'm working on.

I AM...

Vulnerable

Weak at times

Scared

Lacking in confidence

Angry

But

I AM also...

A survivor

Strong

A teacher

A philosopher

An Ethicist

ME

Anne Skorzewski

Escaping Demons

Addiction 162

Black Bird 169

Achilles Heel 170

Safety 171

Storm 172

Torn 173

Back Seat Passenger 175

Numb 177

Demons 181

Alone in the Dark 182

Invisible Wounds 183

Darkness 184

How it Felt when You Said… 187

The Unbroken 188

Stolen 189

Addiction

Choosing one specific thing to write for this book was not easy; my life has had a plethora of ups, downs, traumas and tantrums. I could have focused on one or all of the many accounts of sexual abuse I was subjected to between the ages of three and fourteen. Or perhaps I could have given a detailed account of how my emotionally vacant mother was unable to be the maternal figure this vulnerable little girl needed, which led me to believe I was indeed the inconvenience I grew up believing I was? Or how about one of the many co-dependent relationships I found myself in? Or the moments of terror and fear I felt when a loved one hit me in the face?

Life can feel cruel and vindictive at times, especially to a young and not yet developed psyche. All of the aforementioned situations and experiences are still quite raw to me. I am still working on healing the wounds that still sting from decades of unresolved and overlooked emotions, so to divulge into those topics at this very moment in time, would come from a place of pain, as I am still working on accepting and integrating these memories into my being.

It was only two years ago that I spoke up about all of the accounts of abuse I had suffered in my younger years. I held the torment and discomfort (that at times, I still feel inside today) inside for well over twenty years. I am still very much in the seedling stage of this healing journey. I have been born again, with a chance to re-write my story, and this new story is free from what has kept me going during the first quarter century of my life; this new story is free from addiction.

Growing up I saw my mum and dad both smoke, and it terrified me. *What if they were to die? Who would then be there to keep me safe?* Safety has been and still is a very important aspect I actively work on feeling inside on a daily basis. I learned from a young age that when they were stressed, they smoked more, so it was clear to me that in order for me to feel safe, I should keep them happy by being a good little girl. I observed their smoking activity go up and down rhythmically, like the tides of the sea in accordance with the activity of the moon. If things at home were tense, the smoke filled the house quicker than the days when life felt calm and the horizon was clear.

I believed that I was a contributing factor to the amount that they smoked. If I was bad then they were stressed and they would smoke more. If I was good, they were happier, so they smoked less. By the time I was eight years old, I had had my virginity stolen, and had been sexually assaulted by five different people, but I knew that if I were to tell my parents, or let them know anything about the depth of my pain and anguish, that the stress would cause them to smoke more. Then they would get ill. They might die. And even more bad things would happen to me.

A cycle of self damnation started. I wanted nothing more than to keep the peace at home, but my eight year old brain was struggling to understand all of these overwhelming feelings and process the traumatic events I had been subjected to. So, in my own way, I created a means to cope with these burdens and it was here that my journey with addiction started.

I started earning my keep by doing jobs for my parents from the age of seven onwards. I would frequently wash and hoover their cars, clean the bathroom or even hoover the house in return for a few hours of peace and temporary happiness in the family home, as well as the bonus of a couple of quid, which I chose to exchange for a selection of Pokémon cards and a few bags of sweets.

Pokémon cards are where it started for me. I soon became so excited about the prospect of opening a new packet of cards, to see if I had in fact got one of the few remaining cards I still needed in order for me to complete the set. The anticipation of the weekend, which was always a golden opportunity to earn some cash, to spend it on the things I grew to love, often kept me going during the school week. I would always look forward to the those two precious days where I was free from trying to fit in, and away from the boys who bullied me. I can still remember the excitement, the tingly feelings in my tummy, the raised heartbeat, the beaming grin strapped to my face when I was about to open a new packet of Pokémon cards. It was ecstasy; a temporary vacation from the pain that was growing ever stronger inside.

As I grew up, the cards ceased to bring the same feelings of ecstasy. They were no longer cool, so they failed to provide a cause for bragging or keep me on top of the hierarchy of the playground. Creatively and unconsciously, I found new ways to feel that buzz. My addiction transitioned into things I could shove in my mouth; foods, sugar, chocolate and lots of it.

If there were chocolates or sweets around, and in large quantities, I can guarantee you they wouldn't be around for long. This was a behaviour that was highly encouraged by both of my parents- "a healthy appetite" they called it. Dad and I would often spend time after the chores were done on a Saturday morning, enjoying a triple serving of Frosted Flakes, topped up with full fat milk, and decorated with lavish servings of extra thick double cream. And as if that wasn't enough, we would double dunk custard creams into our hot drinks until we couldn't stomach any more.

I soon found that foods gave a quicker gratifying buzz than the cards ever did and here is where my emotional eating started to form roots. Before long I was not only over eating large quantities of all my main meals, I was also eating plenty of chocolate bars in-between meals too, on the way home from school and after dinner. This behaviour snowballed, and before long I became so embarrassed about the amounts I was able to consume in one sitting, that I started to hide this from my family and my friends, and I was eating in secret.

I can remember- I would have been about eleven years old- I was set with the task of walking to the shop to get my mum some Pepsi Max and a lottery ticket. She gave me money and instructed me under no circumstances were I to spend more than I was told, or we might not have enough left for gas and electric. Luckily for me, I still had some of my own money that I'd kept behind from last weekends' chores, and whilst I was at the shop, I spent the whole £4 on sweets, Penguin bars and pic 'n' mix. I was in e-number heaven!

Not wanting to be seen with an extra bag, I hid the sweets along the side of the house behind an old propped up paving slab, and decorated it with leaves, so that my younger brother and his friends wouldn't find them and rat me out to the masses. The excitement of knowing that I was sneaking around made me feel invisible and powerful. I had a secret, and my own treasure waiting to be devoured the moment I could get the restricted items past customs - this is how it felt being so young and acting so out of align with our family values. It was a risk, but a risk I was willing to take.

I remember eating two whole packets of twelve Penguin bars, in addition to the rest of the goodies I had secretly purchased in only fifteen minutes. The amount of sugar I consumed must have sent my body in to a kind of shock; I remember feeling so full, and so wiped out, that I had to lie down on my bed and soon fell asleep. My bed was usually a place of sobbing to sleep for me. However, on this occasion I was blissfully stuffed; I was happy and had no worries about my safety. The haunting memories of my trauma were no longer there and I drifted off into a sugar induced sleep, waking up a few hours later, still enjoying the taste of chocolate on my lips.

I realised that when I ate a large amount of food and kept it secret, my trauma vanished, so here is where I formed a desire to do whatever I could to stop the trauma from affecting me. When I or the family didn't have money, I would steal chocolate bars from the shops. The thrill was fanatical, but before long the food stopped providing the same emotionally numbing effect that it had done once before. Still wanting my "thrilling fix", I started to use my steadily improving skill in stealing to find my fix elsewhere.

It started with stealing clothes from high street stores and it transitioned quickly. I would try and steal whatever I could, whenever I could. I was the modern day Robin Hood, stealing from the big corporations and giving to the emotionally bankrupt little girl that was screaming out for attention inside my own head. I liked the buzz of stealing, as it helped me to cope with my trauma, but this temporary fix was only ever short lived and those uneasy feelings would quickly return, perpetuating the cycle.

I have been arrested three times for stealing, and each time my parents couldn't understand why I wanted to steal. I didn't steal because I was sexually abused, but at the very core the unresolved emotions left over from these experiences, was the precise reason why I was stealing. The thrill of the potential of getting caught gave me such a distraction from my internal world. It enabled me to build walls and close a door on those emotions, and in turn I closed the door on myself, my needs and my voice.

The addictive and thrill seeking behaviours continued to expand over the next twelve years and took on various forms. The substances often changed, but food was always my biggest problem and the addiction that took the longest to break. Even now I find myself wanting to run to the nearest pick 'n' mix when anything emotionally challenging arises in my life.

I have battled with addictions to caffeine, cocaine, sex, raving and most recently to marijuana. This has probably been the second hardest of them all to kick, as marijuana takes me to a place where I am no longer fazed about the past, present or future; I am neither here, nor there but everything at once. It brings a sense of connection to the disconnected parts of me, and I have used this substance in an attempt to heal myself.

Marijuana took me to the depths of my soul and to some of the darkest thoughts I have ever had, but paradoxically soothed them at the same time. I used it each night so that I would not feel my anger, and to ease my emotional pain. I used it to escape because being me felt so overwhelming. Much like with the Pokémon cards, I fantasised about when I might be able to get high again, and I would work all day with that fantasy at the front of my mind, waiting and itching to get my fix, so I could again for a few hours be transported to my happy place.

Addiction starts with pain and ends with pain; the pain I felt with my parents smoking, led me to hide the pain I felt from my abuse, which led me down a twenty year journey of dodging emotions that I inevitably would one day have to face. But first, I had to run so far away from my authentic self and into a dark, soul- consuming depression in order for me to hit that brick wall. In the narrowing tunnel of self- avoidance, I had no choice but to turn around and face everything I had run from and walk back towards the light.

I am now in counselling for my various counts of sexual trauma, and I am realising just how much I have damned myself through my whole life, but I am embracing this new chapter with open arms. The emotions aren't easy to process, but after each session I feel a little closer to understanding myself. It sure beats running away.

My life now is based on a holistic way of healing through self- affirming mantras, daily yoga and journalling in an attempt to bridge the gap between the pain and the now, giving myself time and space to create a new way of life. I am learning to be patient with my feelings. Some days I sob for the little girl I was ashamed of, and sometimes she shines her light so brightly she uplifts all who she comes into contact with

I am Emily. I am healing. I am not responsible for my trauma and I am not the inconvenience I thought I was... if you say something enough times, you might just begin to believe it!

Emily Joyce

Black Bird

An old friend of mine flew by today

and perched upon the window sill.

Peering in it started tapping

upon the pain of my glassy mind.

Chirping, chippering, and crowing away

at the frailties of a fresh resolve.

Surprising it could fly

considering the heaviness of its song.

A negative refrain full of guilt and blame

in the form of a twilight lullaby,

looking to entice all my hard won insight

into forgetfulness and sleep.

My Black Bird keeps trying to let itself in;

this shadowy herald of addiction and shame

it peeks at me persistently,

while on the inside my white dove coos,

spreads its wings and holds me high.

Sulaiman Mackay

Achilles' Heel

The call to adventure starts
with dusting off the running shoes
especially purchased for the long haul
of the Hero's tricky distance.

The distance will wear away
all the edges from any comfort zone
and tear into every fibre
of my conflicted existence.

When the old injury hinders me
my heel becomes as old as Greek legend.
But it's all happened before;
mythology has already shown us
how to endure through all our ongoing trials
and become reborn.

So I go into the guarded underworld,
into the purifying fire,
into the shadow of the woods,
into the anger, the shame, the guilt
of the addicted hero as he rescues himself
from the ignoble fate of never saving the day.

Sulaiman Mackay

Safety

I've just locked the door,

how's that for a metaphor!

There's nothing I can't just hide away

from the thought of being seen this way.

The lock is automatic

and activated by behaviour

I only want witnessed

by my secret self.

So don't dangle any rattling chain

of keys in front of me,

or hold the power of release

against the comforts of my addiction.

This security is fragile,

but my intent is clear.

Please don't break the door down,

or try to interfere.

Sulaiman Mackay

Storm

Every time I indulge

it takes me one step further away.

Every time I abstain it hurts my brain

and torments my subtle bodies.

I am urged to subdue and deflate.

The turmoil and uneasy moods that pass

with thunderous potential through the night skies

outside my dirty window.

The condensation gathers

on the inside and seeps all over,

soaking everything entirely

with the demands of its attention.

I am wet with thunderous potential.

Here me roar, feel my discharge

as all of my small hairs stand on end

while enlightening the friction

between these dark desires.

Sulaiman Mackay

Torn

Every time I succumb
to the feeling of this addiction,
it inflates the affliction.

Although I am very aware
of how it rips and tears
at the fabrics of my vitality.

Every time I indulge
in the substance of this addiction,
it consumes a little more of me.

Although I am very aware
of how my appetite always
leaves me unfulfilled.

Every time I adorn
the consequence of this addiction,
the masquerade proceeds despite my absence.

Although I am very aware
of how the costume carries me
through the day.

I am completely aware of this addiction
and it always leaves me in two minds,
numb and blind.

Sulaiman Mackay

Back Seat Passenger

I know my own mind.

I can see it,

giving all its power away.

Fleeing in terror from the decadent body,

running in raptures to the decadent body,

impulsed by a feeling it can't control.

 Self-esteem takes a back seat

and lets the body hoon around,

a designated witness so helpless

against the possession of the body

accelerating towards a write-off.

Mind over matter is what the wise like to say.

Mind transcends all matter

and brings liberation at the end of the day.

But matter over mind is what the Addict craves,

matter over mind is to consume the world

while keeping all thoughts of the self away.

Sulaiman Mackay

Numb

My alarm wakens me at 5 am. Another day that feels the same as yesterday. Nothing changes and we repeat the motions until we can no longer maintain them. The mornings are the worst for me. I am so very tired. I wish to sleep and never wake again. You realize your life is in turmoil when your dream state is preferable to your reality. I want to dream for eternity, and I begin to entertain the finality of death.

Unfortunately, there is no time for that. I must get up. There are many people who depend on me. I must wake up my Son, feed him breakfast, brush his teeth, get him dressed, comb his hair, pack his lunch, drive him to school, kiss him and tell him how much I love him. I must get ready for work. I must be the nurse who has his shit together, ready to save a life without pause or hesitation, ready to cater to the needs of others. I must be on time because my co-workers depend on this and my boss demands it. I must smile, make jokes, and laugh at the jokes of others. I must be polite and pleasant. I must exercise and eat healthy. I must keep my body fit and desirable.

Before I can accomplish any of this, I must be numb. I must smoke a piece of heroin or snort a pill before I can feel ready. It is not a matter of getting high or feeling good. It is simply a matter of being numb enough to pretend. To pretend I still have my shit together. To try and glue together my fragmented mental and emotional state. To continue living the lie I tell myself. I must, or others may grow suspicious. They wouldn't understand if they knew my secret. They would judge me and ostracize me. I would lose everything; my career, my child, my life.

I am a drug addict and I am depressed. I just do not realize it yet. Denial is a powerful thing. Human Beings have an uncanny ability to lie to themselves. When the truth hurts we will go to extreme measures to avoid it. I was not that bad. I could quit at any time. I was going to quit next week or the one after. I was still functional; my bills were paid, my child was well cared for, I had friends, I had a girlfriend, people liked and respected me. I was still okay. I wasn't like those other people; the real hardcore addicts.

Self-honesty is the beginning point of any transformation. It was becoming increasingly obvious to me that I had a problem. I would begin to withdraw at work. It was usually in the afternoon that I would begin to ache, sweat, and my skin would crawl. I became more careless with my usage. I would smoke in my car at breaks to stave off the pain. My attendance at work was suffering and my employment was now compromised.

The truth is I wanted to quit. I had tried and failed many times. I kept asking myself *why couldn't I quit? Was I just too weak? Why couldn't I get back to being the person I once was, before all this started? What was missing?*

Everything has its absolute limit. One morning, I was driving my son to school. He was 4 years old. He was in that inquisitive stage of his development. You know, the *why* phase, when they ask why things are the way they are until you can no longer provide an accurate answer. He hated school at that time. Every morning he would cry and beg me not to drop him off. He would ask why he had to go to school. I replied, "Daddy has to work." Why? "Because Daddy has to make money." Why? "So we have a place to live." This continued until I yelled at him to be quiet.

It was in this moment where I had the stark realization; I was miserable, and I hated my life. It is often our immediate answer that is the most honest. I was going through the motions to maintain the status quo. I was working a job I hated. I was dating girl I didn't love. I had lost my sense of purpose, my passion for living. I didn't love myself anymore.

It wasn't the acknowledgment that I was an addict, but that I was unhappy. It was not the denial of my addiction but of my emotions. The drugs were merely a means to further my self-denial. The denial of my pain. A means to keep me numb.

I had a decision to make; life or death. I stopped bullshitting and for the first time I could see clearly where my life was headed if I did not change. I wasn't sure how to proceed. I knew rehab wasn't an option for me. I would potentially lose my Nursing License and my Son. It was not a risk I was willing to take, and I knew it wasn't the answer for me.

I began meditating. I didn't know what I was doing, but I heard it was good for you. I read it could calm the mind and help you relax. I thought it would be useful to help me sleep through the withdrawals. I bought books and downloaded apps. I just started doing it every morning.

Within a few weeks I felt better. I knew it was time. I prepared myself mentally for the physical withdrawals, as best anyone can, but it was the emotional response I was not anticipating. The first day it hit me like a tidal wave. I was sitting naked in my bath tub. I was holding myself, shivering in the hot water, tears streaming down my face. Years of suppressed emotional despair was now flooding to the surface. Amid this pain I thought to myself, *God damn it feels good to feel again. To be human again. To be alive.*

I have been clean ever since and no longer desire drugs. I am not always happy and sometimes I feel sad. I just no longer try to numb the sadness. I embrace it as a temporary part of me. I accept it and love it as I do myself.

It is ironic to me that the secret I kept so well, the one I was once terrified to expose, I now share with you openly and proudly. I could have continued to keep it hidden, but why continue to carry an unnecessary burden? I now see the value in being honest with myself and others. I no longer fear the judgement of others because I accept myself completely. I want you to do the same. I want you to know that it is okay to feel, to struggle with addiction, to not be perfect, to be flawed, to be human. There is beauty in our truth, in our vulnerability, in our emotions. We are all perfectly imperfect.

Dan McGinley

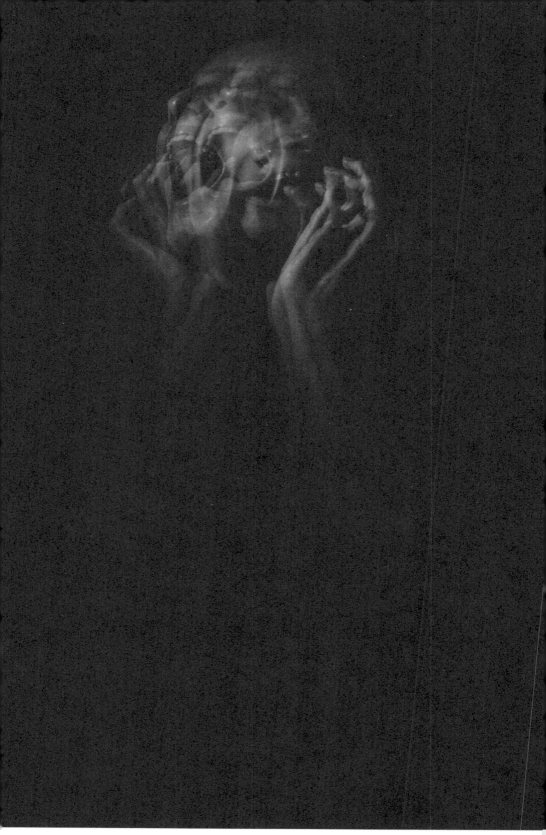

Demons

The fear that churns inside my head

Released while sleeping in my bed

I wake in terror as peaceful dreams

Morph into nightmares and piercing screams

The demons from my past are there

They're all around, they're everywhere

I see danger in stranger's eyes

Their watchful gaze as I pass by

Imagine that they're following me

Reaching out they grab me roughly

In every room within my house

In every noise and every shout

With no safe place to rest inside

I cannot escape, I cannot hide

There's no safe haven I can find

While demons live inside my mind

Karen Horsley

Alone in the Dark

Although its day
It's dark as night
No sun peeks through
No shining light
This smog, like clouds
That reach the ground
Like ash from flames
Fall all around
The power's out
You cannot phone
I need to reach you
I'm scared alone
The world is silent
There is no sound
No one to talk to
My breathing loud
Within the dark
A swirl of grey
I want to know
You're safe today
My eyes are blind
I cannot see
Through this fog
Surrounding me

Karen Horsley

Invisible Wounds

Insidious bleakness

A fog that swirls and shrouds my body and mind

Weighing heavy on limbs

Pressing down with unseen forces

Cold void of trauma and loss

Regrets and self-doubt enveloping my soul

Hope's flame extinguished

Only smoking embers remain

Tight confines of restrictive swaddling

Concealing emotion, impeding action

Suppression of breath

Suppression of self

Ice daggers pierce my heart

Puncture wounds seeping

Invisible pain

As life drips away

Karen Horsley

Darkness

And here it comes again...
The feeling of hopelessness.
The sadness.
The fear that I might never feel differently;
That things may never be any other way.

It is my own doing, of course.
To a degree anyway.
I built this life.
This isolation.
I don't need anybody.
I don't want anybody close to me.
Don't let them in.

Why? you ask.
Self-preservation.
If you don't let them in, they can't hurt you.
But in the process you are hurting yourself.

Days spent curled up in bed.
Doing nothing.
Just watching time go by.
No motivation.
No energy.
No appetite for life.

Oh God when will this end?

I could end it of course. Easily.
The idea is there; the means readily available.
To never feel again?
What a beautiful idea!

But I am rational enough to understand that this is just in my head.
I have a lot to live for; I have a lot to fight for.
The truth is that my fight began a long time ago.
But I had been doing so well for so many years,
Or so I thought.
I think that is why when the darkness got me this time, I never saw it coming.
And boy, did it get me.

It reminded me of how quickly things can change.
How fragile our minds are.
Maybe things didn't change that much at all.
Maybe the darkness I had hidden for so long finally found a way to escape.
The mask I'd been wearing for far too long finally came off.
And for the first time in years I showed my true face to a select few.

Some of them started to keep a distance.
Some of them left altogether.
Some of them I pushed away,
Ashamed of my feelings,
Embarrassed of how I looked; unkempt, unwashed hair, tatty clothes.

The one who had her life together.
The one with the good job.
The one who helped others and listened to them during hard times.

The truth is that yes, it had been there all along.
Buried beneath a busy life.
Never time to sit down and think.
Never allowing myself to process what had happened to me.
What was happening to me.
Keeping myself occupied with work, excessive exercise, businesses, an active social life, men.
But none of them were allowed in.
Not really.

And then it all came crashing down.
And I tried so hard to keep it together.
Don't show weakness.
Don't let them know you're suffering.
And when I did, and they left, it just confirmed everything.

This is why you isolate yourself.
This is why when they ask to see you, you say no.
This is why you spend your weekends alone.
This is why you can't be with anyone.
This is why you will never be with anyone.
This is why you will never be happy.
This is why, even when you have a chance at happiness,
You would rather destroy it before someone else can.

The damage that was done to me, I sometimes worry that it may be irreparable.
It was left to fester for so long.
It is a strange place when your heart feels dead, yet you care so much it aches.
All of the time.

The contempt I hold for myself is deep seated,
Fuelled by someone who did their utmost to
Put me down time and time again from the earliest age.
Instead of nurturing me, he taught me that I was nothing.
That I would always be nothing.
Unworthy of love.
Unworthy of happiness.
Unworthy.

Those are only the echoes of my past of course.
This is not who I am now.
And so I carry on.
Day after day.
Week after week.
I continue to fight to come out of this darkness.
Every. Single. Day.

Yvonne Heiden

have you ever
felt yourself slip into
another dimension and hide
yourself under a blanket
of distress and warp. been warped
into a world i can't
process or understand. what do
i want to be? who am i?
what's going on? and where
do i go in this maze within myself
self who is, self? who is. me? who?
who? is this what
death would feel like? it's evil,
to feel death when you're alive.
–how it felt when you told me you'd rather be dead
than live with the thought that you ever knew me

Gurpreet Raulia

The Unbroken

In the darkness
There is light.
It unfurls
Like the petals of youth
Stolen from the gentle arms of forgiveness.
Alone is the night
That hides beneath quiet waters.
Sombre,
Forgotten,
Solitary
And at one with pain.
Gracious tendrils of kindness from strangers
Grasp and claw
As they reign with power.
Secrets embrace
In the dark,
For sleep will not come.
I envy you;
The unbroken.

Victoria Huntriss

Stolen

by K. Humphries

Metamorphosis

Transformation   197

Redemption   198

Never Enough   201

The Notebook   205

When there is Nothing Left of Me   206

Restoration   209

Sometimes   215

Mitigating Mental Chatter   217

Knowing Your Worth   218

I'm automatically drawn...   220

Depression is...   221

Transformation

I knew I was beginning to develop a habit for over spending, but I couldn't stop it. Each time the pay cheque came in, I'd see it as an opportunity to create a new identity for myself. I'd go out and buy a whole new wardrobe of clothes, shoes, bags and jewellery. It felt like a way to shed the old me and bring in the new one; the improved version.

I never really got myself into financial trouble over it, but when I took stock of my spending and my shopping behaviours, I noticed that this process of continually trying to form a new identity by external means was a pattern I'd repeated many times throughout my life; dieting, hair colour, continually changing jobs, sports, homes. They were all opportunities to 'wipe the slate clean' of the messy person I was, to start over with the intention of leaving that mess behind. But it never worked, and so I found myself continually having to change to escape that mess.

I realised that no external changes were ever going to make a difference- I would never be able to keep up with any 'perfect' outward appearance and that sooner or later I would always 'mess up' or make mistakes because that is the nature of being human. My external changes weren't really transformational at all. They were a means of running from the truth: I am messy. I am chaotic. I do make mistakes. I'm not perfect. The real transformation happened when I began to change my internal wardrobe so to speak. I changed the way I dressed my thoughts and how I felt about myself. I began to reject external ideals and started on a journey towards self-acceptance. And that in itself was the only transformation I ever needed to make.

Transformation is an inner process.

Redemption

Looking back through my journals, I can see the lies that I had always believed about myself. It took me a while to realise that they were lies, but thankfully, when I did, I decided to seek the truth.

I am loved. I am wanted. I am beautiful.

****

I can't remember a time when I really loved myself, my personality and looks. I was called names, as a joke, when I was younger and being a lover of words, they always stuck with me. I even ended up believing them. But I kept this a secret. I decided that I had to do something about it to change the way I felt about myself through controlling what I ate. I would do everything I could to get my weight lower, to a place I felt skinny enough- worthy enough. But that point never came.

Overtime, I became more anxious. My emotions were all over the place. I had awful, negative thoughts about myself, which I masked behind a fake smile. Soon, self-harm became the only relief from that self-hatred; a release of pain in a moment of feeling completely overwhelmed by my constant self-deprecating mind narrative. Each time I self-harmed it got worse, fuelling yet more shame because it left me with scars; scars which only added to the self-hatred, and so the vicious cycle continued.

I remember crying my eyes out for so many hours for countless nights. I thought no one would discover the 'true me'. Throughout all of this, God continued to love me and guide me, to prevent me from going too far. I didn't realise it back then, but I could never hide from Him. He knew my thoughts. I wasn't only hurting myself, but the people around me who watched this process. He cried when He watched me starve and damage myself because I am His precious daughter.

Through developing my relationship with God, I learnt that I didn't have to live with the pain, hatred or hurt that I felt inside of me. God revealed to me that my identity is in Him and that He took time over making me in His image. Changing this mind set didn't happen overnight; it has taken years in fact, and there are still many areas in which I am constantly learning, growing and improving. Learning to receive unconditional love in the places that I hurt the most was a huge challenge, but I couldn't allow myself to live how I was. I felt completely hopeless, lifeless, distant from everyone and fake.

By no means does this mean that I now fully love myself, and sometimes I do fall into old patterns of thinking. But I now have a coping mechanism to help me through the thoughts and prevent my emotions from ruling me. I pray and ask for God to comfort me, to show me His love and I thank Him for how far I have come since, even if I don't always feel it in that moment. I have now come to accept the scars, they show a small part of what I have overcome, and that God heals broken hearts. He is my redeemer.

Charlotte

****

For you created my inmost being: you knit me together in my mother's womb. I praise you because I am fearfully and wonderfully made; your works are wonderful, I know that full well.

Psalm 139:13-14

Never Enough

When I started secondary school, I felt an instant pressure to fit in. I needed to make friends, I needed to be cool. I'd always been a shy child. My mum used to try and sign me up to swimming lessons and Brownies to encourage me to have a social life, but I refused, and it would normally end in tears. My name, Tuesday, was a very unusual one, which attracted unwanted attention. I've heard all the jokes you could possibly think of, and you can imagine the kind of reaction I got from teenage, hormonal kids. Kids can be so cruel. I wouldn't say I was badly bullied, but the constant digs towards my name dented my confidence more.

I remember crying to my mum that I found it so hard to make friends. I didn't know what to talk to people about and when I did try, they would just ignore me or not hear me because I was so quiet. This stayed with me all through my teens and my twenties. It slowly got worse, and I always felt as though I was never enough; not clever enough, not interesting enough, not quick enough to fire back answers when someone insulted me, not funny enough, not eloquent enough and not skinny enough. Just not enough! I have always felt I needed to be accepted, I needed to please people. Sometimes this meant forgoing what I truly wanted to do for what I thought others wanted me to do.

I was twenty six when I fell pregnant with my first baby. I knew from that point that I needed to force myself to make friends, not only for my own sake and my own sanity, but I knew I needed to be a good role model for my baby. He needed to see me making friends and chatting freely to people to enable him to be a sociable person. My husband and I joined the NCT and booked onto one of their antenatal courses. This is where I met five wonderful ladies who have become my mummy tribe. We have shared so much together, and I believe they have shaped the way I parent my children. These ladies were the beginning of my journey.

Since then I've pushed myself into difficult situations. Forcing myself to talk to people, making conversations with the mums at school, setting up play dates for us to meet with our children, even when it was the most uncomfortable feeling and when all I wanted to do was bow my head and not make eye contact. I have also completed the first year of a counselling course, something I never thought I would do, before realising that my heart wasn't in it, but I have taken many of the skills with me and I shared some of my inner most thoughts to nine strangers on a regular basis over the course of that year.

I have gone on to have two more children and have met many people from different walks of life along the way. Some I feel more comfortable with than others. Sometimes I still have those feelings that create a tight chest and butterflies in my tummy. I still sometimes dread being in a situation where I'm alone with one person and having to make conversation, but I push myself outside of my comfort zone. About a year and half ago someone close to me tried to define me in one word. A word that was negative and disapproving. This triggered something in me that forced me to connect with myself, and made me question *who am I?* And it sent me down a road of self-discovery.

After much reflection, I have realised that you can't always please everyone. I know in my heart that I am a kind, genuine person. I'm not perfect, but none of us are and every day I try to do better. I try to make a difference, but I've realised I don't need to prove myself to anyone anymore. You can either choose to see the goodness in me or not, and if you don't then actually the problem lies with you. I now allow myself to acknowledge a negative reaction or negative opinion towards me, but I don't allow it to affect me and I no longer waste energy worrying about it. I move on in the knowledge that that person is obviously unhappy about themselves or their lives. It's not my feeling, it's theirs, and I now feel free.

I am enough.

I've also discovered that it is possible to have different levels of connections with different people and that's ok. That's normal. It doesn't mean there's something wrong with me just because I can chat more with some people and less with others. I realise now that as an adult it is much harder to find true friends, someone you connect with and are truly comfortable with and if you are lucky enough to find these connections, they must be treasured. I have been extremely blessed to meet some very special women since beginning my journey. All of them are an inspiration to me and I am very blessed to have them in my life. I am so glad I pushed myself on this road to discover who I am. I'm still learning and still navigating my way around, but I am definitely more confident and hope that my new career as a children's yoga teacher can help many children feel important, confident and self- assured. I am passionate about encouraging the next generation to be kind, empathetic, thoughtful human beings.

Tuesday

The Notebook

When I was younger, I used to buy new notebooks with interesting regularity. I absolutely loved the idea of the newness, the fresh, clean unadulterated pages. It was like starting over; a fresh start. It would be even better if I had a new pen or pencil too.

I would open the notebook with a great sense of excitement. I usually wrote my name first, as neatly as humanly possible, and then whatever else I had on my mind to write. But I would often struggle with what to write and how to express myself on those blank pages. *What did I even have to say?*

Eventually, as I always knew would happen, I would write something I didn't like or 'mess up' my handwriting. And that would always be the end of the new beautiful notebook! There was no way I could continue because it was no longer 'perfect' as I saw it. Quite often, at this point, I would scribble and scrawl over the pages, as I was so annoyed with myself for spoiling my book.

As I look back now, I can see what was happening. The notebooks were a manifestation of my struggles as a young girl. Every time I bought a new book it was a chance to show myself that I was 'good', 'worthy', 'enough' and each time I 'failed' to keep the pages clean, neat and tidy I was proving to myself that I wasn't enough.

Now when I write in one or other of my books, (I have several on the go) I can write in them without any worry of 'spoiling' them and enjoy them for what they are- a place to make notes! Sometimes I choose to write neatly and other times I literally scribble down what I want or need to remember. The most important thing to me now is the content of the pages; the knowledge, the revelations, the outworking of what drives me to write, learning more and more about who I am. I'm enjoying the process of self-discovery and after many years of learning to heal those wounds, I now love this journey that I am on.

My pages aren't neat like my life isn't; it can be messy and seemingly in the wrong order, but there is so much more fun and reality in the freedom of the scrawl. This is where life and growth really happens- in the mess and the chaos!

Kate Harpum

When there is Nothing Left of Me

What can I give

When there is nothing left of me?

When my caverns echo only sounds

That you've imposed on me.

When you've devoured

The flesh of my soul

With the unsatiable hunger

Of a grave digging ghoul

And taken even the bones of me.

No longer even a corpse

But a long lost memory

Of somebody I used to be.

Who Am I

When there is nothing left of me?

Except ashes and dust.

Now that I am gone

And you've satisfied your lust

For spirit gorging.

How do I begin

To restore what I've forgotten

When what I was

Is now so rotten.

The land and sea

That once was me

Now an uninhabitable land.

Barren.

A blanket of darkness

Comes to tuck me in

For one final goodnight,

But as I close my eyes in surrender

A glimmer of light.

The Sun is rising.

My tears fall.

Water and sunlight

Is how I'll grow it all.

My tears and pain

Provide the rain

For regrowth.

Up I rise

From the seed that was left of me.

Grown again

Echoing only the sounds that make up

Me.

Maria Alfieri

Restoration

I always felt different from as far back as I can remember. The odd one out. Complicated. Not sure how or where I fitted in. I was swamped with a general feeling of being 'wrong' in some way, and life always felt like an uphill battle. I didn't even feel like I belonged in my own family, like it was a mistake that I was there; the ugly duckling amongst a family of swans. I decided somewhere along the way that it was probably better to be someone, anyone, other than me, and so I embarked on a journey of discovering who I thought I 'should' be and what I thought everyone else wanted me to be, in the hope to finally find a sense of belonging.

I remember the initial feeling of happiness at the prospect of starting secondary school; I was starting afresh and hoped that things could get better and that I might find what I'd been looking for. But once the enormity of having to be there for the next five years set in, I quickly started to slip into depression. I can still sense the anxiety and nausea I would experience nearly every morning, desperate for a way to get out of going. I was so relieved on the days I managed to convince my mum that I wasn't well enough for school, although it didn't take long before I started panicking about having to go back. Even when I was genuinely ill and felt awful, I was still happier being at home for the day than being well.

As I got older, I started comparing myself to other girls; slimmer, prettier girls and started to believe that I was ugly as well as useless, so my body image became a real issue on top of everything else. I thought that maybe if I had the same haircut, or if I wore the clothes that someone else was wearing, I would look and feel different, and might even find a place to belong somehow. No matter how hard I tried it never worked. I was exhausted.

The more I disliked, or more specifically hated myself, the angrier and more unpleasant I became. Once I was in my mid to late teens, I realised that I did have something that made me feel better about myself; the attention of boys. It made me feel good to be noticed and gave me a sense of value. I craved the attention so much that I started going out of my way to get it. I had no respect for myself whatsoever, and I was desperately lonely, sad and heartbroken. It became an awful, vicious, self -destructive cycle. At the time I don't think I realized that what I was doing was so damaging to me, but I had no concept of any other way to behave and it just became worse as time went on.

I started to think that once I found a good man and had my own home and children, all would fall into place, and that that was the answer. How wrong I was! Nothing externally could 'fix' me because I was broken inside. There was nothing fundamentally wrong with me, just my perception of me. I allowed others to contribute to how rubbish I felt about myself and believed anything negative that was said. I filtered out the good stuff and compliments made me feel so uncomfortable because I didn't believe I was worthy. When everything else in my life seemed out of control, I turned to the one thing I could control; my weight.

I would do everything I could to keep my weight down, sometimes only eating a bowl or two of cereal a day. Other days I would eat rubbish like cakes, crisps and chocolate and then eat nothing at all until I felt I had rectified my bad eating, or at least somehow 'made up' for it. My weight started to yo-yo, and for years I followed that pattern. I would go from being so in control of everything I ate and not allowing myself anything yummy, right to the other end of the scale and eating everything in sight and not caring, (although I did really). The battle in my mind waged constantly. I associated my value with the way I ate and looked. When I was 'in control' and thin I felt worthy and when I wasn't I was disgusted with myself.

It seemed to me that everyone had it together except me (which I now realise was not/is not the case) but I couldn't understand why. I felt like a frightened child most of the time. I was paranoid about what others thought of me, I constantly apologised for myself and generally lived in fear. I felt so confused, as I was a loving person and wanted so much to love those around me, but what seemed to come out all the time was anger!

Looking back, I honestly don't know how I survived certain times of my life.

Some days were black from the moment I opened my eyes in the morning to the time I went to sleep - nothing but darkness, no light and no hope. The only thing that gave me the tiniest bit of sparkle was the thought of taking something, or the chance to get drunk because then I could go to the land of pretend. But essentially that would only make things worse in the long run. It was a quick fix and when the effects wore off, the whole process would start over again. Loneliness returned, along with fear and rejection. The pain tore away at my mind. *What the f**k was the point of any of this? What the f**k was the point of me?* I hated everything about my existence.

It wasn't until I had my first child that the word depression was used about me. I heard the midwife whispering to my then husband. She told him that he should keep an eye on me, as she thought I may have postnatal depression. I was incensed! *How dare she? Did she not know how much I wanted my baby and that I loved him with all my heart?* I was so angry, and sadly my husband was the one who took the hit. I was hurt and confused and ANGRY! That seemed to be my default setting - angry, unless of course everything was running smoothly, and I felt in control, which obviously was incredibly rare with a new born baby and depression.

How could I admit that I was feeling depressed when I had everything that I had ever wanted? I had a lovely husband, our own home and a new born baby who I loved with all my heart. If I told anyone I was depressed, they would think I was selfish and didn't appreciate what I had, and the truth was I felt so, so lucky. So lucky in fact it scared me. *What if I messed up? What if it was all taken away from me?* I didn't deserve everything I had because I wasn't worthy; I was stupid, I was ugly and useless. I was tormented in my head 24/7 and there was no escape. All I wanted was a switch behind my ear that I could just turn off, so I could get some peace. In the absence of that switch I would sleep instead. Sleep gave me rest bite from the endless whirring in my head, but it was just never enough, and I eventually didn't want to wake at all.

I can't remember when I finally went to the doctors to ask for help, but when I did, they gave me anti- depressants. I was caught between relief and mortification that I couldn't cope on my own, which just confirmed to me all the things I already knew about myself; that I was a total and utter waste of space. I constantly felt sad that my husband and children had to put up with me and what a crap deal they all had. More than once I decided that they would be better off without me. I truly believed that and would often tell my husband that I should leave, but he would convince me that was not true. Eventually though, my marriage broke down, and then I experienced the agony of divorce and the pain of seeing my children so hurt. It almost killed me at times; I couldn't even keep my husband.

Slowly, bit by bit, I began to listen to the positive things my friends and family were telling me, and I started to believe it. Fast forward to now. I no longer feel like the lost, broken, hurting 'waste of space' that I used to because I'm not, and in fact, I never was. I am Kate and I love my life. I don't mean that my life has suddenly become perfect; it hasn't. I just shifted my mindset; I believe in me now. I believe I have worth and value. It's incredible what a difference that makes to the way you live your life. It also makes a difference to the way you see others too, looking for their value rather than just seeing their faults. Liking me has made me like others, and I try to see the good in others even if I must look a bit harder sometimes. I know that when the darkness comes, whether it lands for a minute, an hour, a day or even a week, it can't stay because it isn't who I am, and it is not what I choose. I choose the light and I choose life. I am constantly discovering more about myself and who I am to others.

For me taking anti- depressants is still something I need to do. I have been taking them for the best part of seventeen years, with the odd short break in between. I have times when I think I would really like to come off them, but when I have tried it hasn't gone well, so I continue to take them. What is the stigma attached to taking medication for our mental health? Why is it any different to taking medication for diabetes, or hay fever, or any other physical condition? I don't know, but what I do know is that taking my medication helps me to pursue what I want in life and get the most out of it. We only get one life and it should be lived to the full and if taking medication helps me to do that, then I will.

That voice in my head that used to tell me how useless I was only had control and influence in my life because I allowed it. It has taken a long time for me to change my inner voice. I still hear some unhelpful negativity at times, but I think we all do. The difference now is, I don't let the negative thoughts control me; I hear them and know that they'll do nothing but hinder my journey to peace and freedom. And so, I put them to one side, tuning into my real wants and needs, so that I can live a life of abundance.

Kate Harpum

Sometimes

Sometimes, I just wish somebody, anybody, would notice me... I can't believe I used to think this way; that I quietly hid alone in my despair hoping that someone might use their mind reading skills to dispel my isolation and misery.

The truth is no one can read your mind. You have to open up. You have to talk. And when you do you'll realise that people are a lot more understanding and compassionate than you thought. The judgement you fear is blocking your progress.

Do not believe the lies your mind tells you. We've all experienced discomfort, anguish, pain, loss, grief, doubt, guilt, shame, depression and anxiety in some form; it is what makes us human. When we all come together to acknowledge this we automatically transport ourselves out of our isolation and find ourselves amongst the community we have craved for so long.

We find a place to belong through honest conversation.

Mitigating Mental Chatter

When that inner critic starts to shout, which it quite often does, you need to find a way to make peace with it. It requires determination. It requires effort. Mitigating mental chatter isn't easy, especially not at first. But with practise and resolve you can learn to hear those negative thoughts but not let them control you, or dominate how you feel about yourself and how you therefore interact with the world. Be kind and patient. Be gentle. Acknowledge those dark thoughts and then let them float on by. Ask for a Power greater than you to take them away. Just stay mindful. Be present. Find tools relevant to you, and surround yourself with the right support. A fundamental part of good self-care is learning to recognise the voice of the inner bully and intercepting it when you hear it.

Knowing Your Worth

I've always struggled with self-worth. I felt easily dismissed as a child. Over-looked. Un-noticed. My value was based entirely on being a 'good' and obedient girl. Intelligent. Able to follow instructions and rules. My worth was something that I had to earn through achievement or subservience.

When I had children of my own, I feared that I wasn't worthy of their love; not because I am a terrible mother to them, in fact, I think I'm quite possibly the opposite, but because I didn't know or value my own worth, and so that fear bled into everything I did.

I channelled all of my energy into compensating for my unworthiness of being their mother, which in fact only caused them to begin to take me for granted. I'd always encouraged my children to 'do their best' and 'be themselves'. I was constantly telling them I was proud of them, especially when I witnessed their kindness towards others and let them know daily that they were loved.

But it gradually dawned on me that it didn't matter how much I told them that they were valued if I didn't work on valuing myself and recognising my own worth; children always see the truth no matter how hard we think we disguise it and they certainly model behaviour. I realised that my children would never be able to truly value themselves if I didn't value myself.

I remember catching myself saying, 'I'm just your mum', completely (and unknowingly) dismissing myself, my role and inadvertently teaching my kids that being a parent was a 'just' – signifying some sort of inferiority. And then I thought about all the things that role includes; carer, teacher, counsellor, night nurse, cook, cleaner, artist, musician, taxi... the list is endless. "But I don't get paid for the work I do," was another phrase I'd catch myself saying, but then realised that not everything we do of value comes with a price tag.

I thought about the work I do as a volunteer, and all the other things I do for 'free' and decided to use that to my advantage to teach the children about the importance of giving ourselves and our time to others, about sometimes being selfless whilst knowing our boundaries, highlighting my worth and theirs within the family and wider community.

I'm glad that I came to recognise my worth sooner rather than later; the greatest way we can teach our kids to learn to love, respect and value themselves is to be the example. It doesn't mean we have to be perfect at it, and we certainly need them to know that mistakes are a part of life from which we grow. But telling your children that they should value themselves and know their own self -worth is only half of the battle. The other half is knowing and valuing yourself.

"I'm automatically drawn to think the absolute worst of myself. But sharing this with others, and knowing that other people do this too somehow makes me feel better. It reassures me that I'm not broken in anyway. And because I know that I'm not broken, I am much more able to challenge the mind narrative when it starts to bombard me with a commentary that I know is absolute bullshit."

"For me, depression is more than just feeling low. It is feeling trapped in a black hole where everything loses meaning and life seems pointless. It feels suffocating. Overwhelming. I didn't even realise that I was depressed, until I'd read a book about depression and could relate to many of the symptoms being discussed. I over ate to escape the darkness when it came to gain some temporary relief from my discomfort. I guess they fed into each other- the overeating and the depression, but once I understood that I had depression and was using food to self-medicate, tackling the disordered eating became a lot easier, as I was able to approach my recovery from a place of understanding."

Hope

Claire 225

Anxiety and Depression 233

Life Can Change in a Moment 240

The Better Way to Life 245

Gratitude for Bodies 251

Moses 252

In The Wake of the Walking Wounded 256

Parenting and Mental Health 263

Kate and Her Wolves 267

Sometimes You Can't See the Wood for the Trees 269

Living on the Surface 271

Imagine 273

Step into the Sunshine 275

Final message 277

Claire

The 10th January 2013 is a date I will never forget; the day I was diagnosed with breast cancer at the age of thirty two.

I got married in my early thirties and we were so lucky to fall pregnant within three months of trying. We bought our first home shortly after getting married. I remember us opening the door to our new home with friends helping us move in and my husband and I sharing secret glances and smiles, as we knew that I was a few weeks pregnant. Our son arrived after a relatively smooth pregnancy and luckily a very quick labour. Life was pretty perfect! We were so happy and already started planning our next child, thinking that when our son turned one, we would 'crack on' with baby number two.

One Friday morning, shortly after I had finished breastfeeding my son, I was in the shower and felt a big lump in my right breast. I thought it might be mastitis, although I had no pain, which I heard was common with mastitis. I called the GP who advised me to try to express and if the lump hadn't gone by the weekend to call back. I called the GP back on the Monday as the lump was still there. I was seen by a lovely GP on the Tuesday. She was calm, friendly and thorough. I remember her describing the lump as firm and warm. I was quickly seen within two days at a local hospital.

A close friend came with me and entertained my son whilst I had a check-up. This involved an aspiration, mammogram and biopsy. I clearly recall the specialist who was doing the biopsy comment, 'there's the swine' as he took an ultrasound under my armpit. My husband came with me for the results that afternoon. As they called my name to go into the room, the consultant walked in with two Breast Care Nurses. I thought, "This is it, how bad is it?"

There is no easy way to tell someone that they have cancer. The kindness and care that I have been given by the various medical specialists has been truly outstanding. I was advised that I needed to start treatment as soon as possible -most likely a single mastectomy and then chemotherapy potentially followed by radiotherapy. I was sent off for a variety of extra scans – CT scans, MRIs and a bone scan. After all the scans came back, it was confirmed that the lump was big – 48mm, there was a positive lymph node and the cancer was HER2 positive, which is an aggressive cancer.

One of the hardest things with a cancer diagnosis is telling other people. Telling people was awful, I hated it. My parents live in another country, so I had to tell them by phone. They were amazing – they stayed positive and gave me strength and reassurance that I could get through this. We all know so many people who have been affected by cancer. Most people were incredibly supportive and were there for me more than I could have imagined. Others just didn't know what to say or said something totally unhelpful, like how their Auntie's neighbour's friend had the same thing and they died a few months ago! Now when others tell me about their diagnosis, or that of a loved one, I always listen deeply and try to be positive, as I remember how hard I found it to tell others and then deal with their reaction.

Our close friends were getting married one week after my diagnosis. At that stage, I didn't know exactly what I was dealing with or what the treatment plan would be. My husband and I decided not to tell our friends as it wasn't the right time and I wasn't ready. That wedding made me realise how strong I could be. I put my brave face on and chose to ignore what was happening in my boob. I enjoyed a happy day with two people that I loved.

Once all the results were in, the Oncologist's advice was to start primary chemotherapy as soon as possible to try to shrink the lump as much as possible and minimise the spread. I instantly trusted my Oncologist. He was honest, clear and involved me in the decisions around my treatment as much as possible. He always smiled when he saw me get my note book out with lists of questions asking about risks, options, medical research and studies and whatever was on my mind in general! Everyone deals with cancer in their own way. Mine was to read a lot and try to make informed decisions on the medical treatment that I was about to face. A question I used with medical specialists throughout my treatment was, "If I was your wife or daughter, what would you suggest I do?" I always found this gave me a more personal and honest answer.

I tried to avoid doing too much online research and reading of blogs, as many just made me sad and think that the only outcome was that I was going to die. Instead, I found solace and practical advice reading information booklets and some amazing books on real life stories as well as lifestyle and diet tips. I found MacMillan's information booklets incredibly useful to understand so many things from diagnosis, treatment, helping me to get through the treatment and then starting to move on with life after treatment. I realised that looking after my mental health would be just as much a part of this journey as looking after my physical health.

One of the first things that I struggled to deal with once I was diagnosed was whether my son would develop cancer. I just couldn't get my head around the fact that he could be OK when I had cancer and had been breastfeeding him. I was assured by my specialists that he was fine and tried really hard to believe this. A work colleague who is a doctor gave me some research information on the topic years after my diagnosis to reassure me he would be OK. Acts of unprompted kindness like that have really helped.

Some of the effects of chemotherapy are like having the flu, so my husband suggested that I treat these effects as if I did have the flu. That approach worked for me –it made it much less scary and manageable. I started chemo in February – not long after getting all the test results back. One of my brothers advised that I should try to take each day and stage of treatment at a time, treating each one as a single hurdle and then to focus on the next one. If I didn't do that, I think cancer would have been totally overwhelming and would have consumed me. Chemo lasted about four months. One thing I read about was "apoptosis" where chemo makes the cancer cells die. I remember sitting in the hospital chair whilst the drugs were going through my body and trying to visualise the cancer cells bursting and disappearing!

I tried the cold cap which can help minimise hair loss by freezing your head basically! But my hair was still falling out in clumps, so I decided to get my husband to shave it off. He did this in the dining room in front of our son who was around eight months old at the time. We had big smiles on our faces, hoping that he would see what we were doing and wouldn't be scared when he then saw me with no hair. I managed to get through this without crying.

I never realised how much losing my hair – literally everywhere – would make me look so different. I didn't take to wearing a wig so opted for headscarves instead. People can't help but stare. My favourite comment was when we went to a christening and a friend's daughter said, "Wow cool, Claire has come dressed like a pirate." A sense of humour was definitely needed at times! But there were many times when I couldn't bear to look in the mirror, couldn't get myself out of bed and everything hurt. Sometimes these lows went on for a day, sometimes longer. I normally found the strength to carry on by trying to focus on that next hurdle and my gorgeous son, husband, family and close friends.

Our friends and family rallied around us and really took such amazing care of us – cooking, arranging a cleaner, looking after our son, taking me for treatment, visiting me... the list was endless. I found it incredibly hard to ask people for help. My family helped out whenever they could which was tricky as they live all over the country and some live abroad. They also sent gifts and useful things when they couldn't be with me in person to remind me they were thinking of me. Some friends would turn up at our door with freshly cooked food or to take my son out for a couple of hours so that I could sleep or just rest. I used this time to sleep or put on some chilled music to try to zone out from the whole situation and just be quiet.

I visited an amazing local cancer charity called the Olive Tree for relaxation and massage which really helped me switch off and have some "me" time. I used a counsellor as well. It was definitely helpful and helped me refocus my negative thoughts into 'self-care' - a principle that has stayed with me and I always try to apply this in my life now. I've recently found out more about counselling and mental wellbeing support that is available such as the charity MIND and the NHS service "Time to Talk" – there are a lot of options to get help and talking about mental health and wellbeing is the first step.

During chemotherapy, I had several different Oncologists as they swapped clinics. One was so positive and reassuring during my chemotherapy. She was confident the lump would shrink significantly and said it may even disappear during chemo. It didn't. I remember being so cross with her at the end of chemo when the lump was still big and I felt she'd given me false hope. As time passed,

I realised that I was being very unfair. She wasn't a magician, she couldn't 'fix' me and was just trying to help me stay positive and get through the treatment.

After chemo I asked to have a double mastectomy even though a single mastectomy was the specialists' advice. The specialists let me proceed with the double mastectomy. In my mind, I wanted to take any chance possible to minimise the cancer spreading or returning. It was a big decision and one I am still glad that I made. I was never a busty girl, but the impact mentally of having the double mastectomy was huge. The operation went smoothly and I was very well looked after in the hospital in order to manage the pain and recovery. I then had some lovely nurses come and visit me at home to tend to my wounds and empty my drains. I found it quite odd having drains under my arms/chest area and having to carry the drains in bags on my shoulders! The drains stayed in for over two weeks and when the nurse had to pull them out, it was sore. The drains had started to think that they were a part of my body, so they needed a strong tug to get out!

Looking back, my husband and close family and friends never looked at me differently – well they didn't show it in their facial expressions. I remember looking in the mirror after my mastectomy – I was bald, my skin looked really grey and I was very thin. It made me realise that people loved me for me and not for how I looked!

I decided to have reconstruction, as being totally flat chested did make me feel less feminine. It was a long process, but for me, it was totally worthwhile. Getting some shape back made me feel more confident.

I was on a drug called Herceptin for one year which involved going to the hospital every three weeks for the intravenous medication. Luckily, it didn't have too many side effects, but the on-going trips to the hospital weren't easy mentally. I was put on a drug called Tamoxifen right after my mastectomy and advised to remain on it for ten years to help reduce the chances of cancer coming back.

Tamoxifen can make me tired and at times it feels like a fog over me and I can't think clearly. But I try to reframe it; that these feelings and emotions can also just be from normal life and not just the drug. These side effects have eased a lot over time and happen much less frequently.

Another thing I've struggled with since having cancer is the fact that it has impacted on how many children we can have. I'm from a big family of five kids and really wanted my son to have siblings. I always wanted three children, but my husband and I settled that two kids would be great. The cancer I had was moderately responsive to hormones, so I was advised to stay on Tamoxifen for at least two years before having a break and "finishing my family".

The research on Tamoxifen changed around the time of my diagnosis; it showed that staying on the drug for ten years reduced the risk of recurrence significantly. It is dangerous to get pregnant on Tamoxifen with a high risk of deformities for the baby. At the two-year point, I was advised that given the type of cancer I had, it would be wiser to stay on it for five years and then "finish my family". I'd be in my late thirties by then, so should still be able to have more children. I have had three different opinions from three Oncologists over the years on the risks of coming off Tamoxifen and trying for another child. I realise that there can be no guarantees, and there is very little data or medical research to help me make a decision.

I've had some tests and scans to see how my body is now and then my husband and I will talk to a fourth Oncologist about the results and our options. My heart says, "Go for it, have another child" and my head says, "Don't go near that, you're lucky to be alive and have a full life." I know we will make a decision that is right for our family. Even if we are able to have another child, if the cancer came back again due to me getting pregnant, I'm not sure if I could mentally cope with that when I already have a wonderful husband and an amazing son.

I have told my son that we'd love another child, but there is a strong chance it won't be possible. His reply humbled me – "I would love a brother or sister mummy but if we can't, I'll be OK." There is no hole in my life and the term "finish my family" is the wrong way to look at things - life just hasn't turned out as I hoped. We are a very happy family of three, and I intend to be around for as much of it as I can.

When I get a new ache or change in my body my mind races to "cancer". I always try to use the "give it two weeks" rule, and if the change doesn't go away in that time, call my GP straight away. Early diagnosis is key.

I get a lot of strength and hope from my faith and our local church and community who have really supported our family. I like the principle behind mindfulness – I really try to focus on the here and now rather than think back to the past or try to predict the future.

Cancer in a way was the worst but also best thing that happened to me. I am now much better at not "sweating the small stuff" and focussing on what really matters to me. My body looks different but bizarrely, I'm more confident and happy in my own skin now than I ever have been.

Claire

BE LOVE

Inspire

Connection

...han ...ulture.

...ll ...d

WE ARE THE ONES WE'VE BEEN WAITING FOR.

Everyone will be alright ♡

Where there is ♡ There is life.

YOU ARE ENOUGH

Be A PART of the SolUTion "That MEANS you too!!"

be proud to be YOU!!!

Live to love! ♡

I will n silent fo sake of at the c what's

NTU AYS.

l ove

Stay Strong. Love each other !

Now that its done — Lets move forward as 1

I am grateful for you

L♡ WIN THE

ce

...ine Evans

STAND UP WITH AND FOR EACH OTHER

I AM NOT AFRAID

—

TURN THE TIDE

RIGH defeate stro evil

LOVE + LIGHT

the possibility of change! ♡

We are still here!

Freedom and Love ♥

SUS

S HATE! STOP THE VIOLENCE!

...ONESS PLEASE ♡ ♡ ♡

el ga su

together

Do all the good you can for all the people you can for as long as you can.

The Sun come out tomorrow

Anxiety and Depression

I had a very happy childhood. I was always very active, a dare devil and even a bit of tom boy. I had lots of friends but always felt a little different from the other girls; their gossip and conversation never interested me.

I was always mentally exhausted at the end of a school day. I think even then, the signs of an underlying tendency to be anxious and depressed were there but didn't really surface until they were significantly triggered at the age of thirteen, where I felt I lost all sense of security and stability.

We moved away from our family home (and my friends). I instantly disliked our cold new house. It was only a few miles away, but to me it felt a million miles away from my comfort zone and my happy days of childhood. When my older siblings moved out, I felt an unbearable sense of emptiness, having shared a bedroom with my middle sister for thirteen years. It suddenly seemed that everything was changing, and I didn't feel at all comfortable with it. For a short period my best friend came to live with us, which temporarily gave me some comfort again, but the panic attacks had already started, and I had no idea what they were or why they were happening to me.

The first panic attack was so intense that I thought I was going to die! I suddenly had a racing heart. I couldn't control my breathing. My lips and fingertips were tingling. And the sweat poured from me. I felt as though something awful was about to happen and eventually I blacked out. It was a terrifying experience for anyone, let alone somebody of such a young age. Following this was months, years even, of medical investigations into unknown stomach pains and extreme anxiety.

Friends didn't understand what had happened to me, and so I stopped being invited to go out to do the things which typical teenagers do. I had become terrified of anything which may bring on a panic attack and started to over think everything. Embarrassed and ashamed, I found myself writing little notes of encouragement to myself to keep in my school bag, which I could read as and when the anxiety would get the better of me in those long and lonely school days.

I had many doctors appointments (I can still feel the anxiety and butterflies when sitting in the doctors waiting room) and memories of so -called professionals prescribing stomach calming medication. It was even suggested that I may be pregnant, even though I was still a virgin! I was sent for all sorts of intrusive examinations, with no reassurances. My anxiety issues had been mentioned, but at no point was this addressed; they focused instead on possible physical problems, rather than trying to help me cope with my overwhelming feelings of anxiety- the physical symptoms being a side effect of this rather than the other way around!

Every day became a secret. An exhausting challenge; get up, get dressed and go to school in the sincere hope that I would be okay and that nothing would provoke any kind of anxiety in me. Little did I know that something as innocent as watching an educational video in an English lesson, would leave me physically shaking uncontrollably with fear, and feeling physically and mentally drained. Viewing the violence of an historical battle (witnessing violent killings, when every ounce of my soul was craving comfort and reassurance at this time) left me shaking and feeling uncontrollably anxious to the point of total physical exhaustion. Nobody else seemed to be bothered in the slightest by the film we had just viewed, and so I had to hide my embarrassing symptoms of this thing, which was eating me up inside.

Current affairs at the time were far too scary for me to even comprehend, so I avoided being in the room when my parents watched the news on TV. But during a Chemistry lesson at school one day somebody mentioned the threat of war; bombings and chemical attacks from Saddam Hussein. My mind ran with the terror of this for months, having nightmares and extreme anxiety about the possibility of living in a war- torn country. I catastrophised but was too afraid to admit my worries to anybody and too young and unsupported to rationalise. As I became more fearful, the anxiety only worsened.

Suddenly I found myself too scared to go out; afraid to do the things all my friends of a similar age were doing. My comfort zone was at home and even there I was experiencing up to fifteen panic attacks a day! I had no one to talk to and very little support. My parents tried their best, but in those days there was little awareness, information, or support for this type of thing. I just knew that when I was in panic mode, I didn't want my mum to leave my side.

Some sort of self-preservation mode kicked in; I stopped eating any foods which I thought might make me ill. I wouldn't eat any food prepared by anyone other than myself, and I became obsessed with checking use by dates on anything I consumed. Eggs, seafood and some meats were absolutely off of the menu. I stuck with 'safe' foods such as crisps and bread (although half way through eating, I'd go back to the kitchen to check the use by dates one more time). The thought of being ill in any way, or not in control terrified me beyond belief. It didn't help that my parent's relationship had been rocky for quite some time. That unsettled me further. I hid some of my anxiety and obsessive behaviours from them by trying to maintain some 'normal' activities with my peers, as I didn't want to cause them any further and unnecessary concern. But by this point my Obsessive Compulsive Disorder was completely controlling me.

After sitting my mock exams separately from everyone else, I stopped socialising entirely, my friends started to drift, and my parents finally split up under very volatile circumstances. Following their break-up, I endured six months of living in a hostel with my heartbroken mother, waiting for a new home. Once we were re housed, I experienced my first overpowering symptoms of depression. I'd finish a day at work and go home to sleep. And I just wanted to sleep all of the time. I was seventeen, beautiful, with a body to die for, but I still had the fear in me and I felt tired. All of the time. And I had no idea why. My body felt heavy and my attention span and interest in work, relationships, friendships and life seemed to fade. I began to use food as a comfort and very quickly gained four stone in weight. Comments such as "just cheer up" and "what have you got to be miserable about" made me feel even more ashamed and angry. Why didn't people understand that I had an illness which wasn't my fault? Would these people have the same disrespectful, sceptical opinion of something like dementia? Just because you can't see it, does not mean that it doesn't exist.

There were extreme highs and lows at this time; I experimented with illegal drugs, experiencing the incredibly awful come down symptoms, which I believe are bad enough for anybody who does not already suffer with any mental illness, let alone for someone already struggling mentally. I lived recklessly, promiscuously and put myself into some dangerous situations. I drank to excess and spent money like it was going out of fashion; a lost soul, searching for something unknown.

I experienced OCD again, I also suffered a period of PTSD following a harrowing event in the past whereby a next-door neighbour had tried to murder his wife and children. He had set fire to the house after stabbing his partner and left them all to perish. Myself, my mum and my boyfriend at the time assisted in rescuing them from the burning house. Thankfully, they all survived, but for me the memories very much lived in my mind. I developed severe OCD with anything which could potentially cause a fire (in some cases, I'd drive fifteen miles back home to check that I'd switched something off). I had some extreme paranoid thoughts, where by at one point, I was even terrified that I was going to somehow harm a loved one in my sleep! My exhausted mind was working overtime to try to make sense of things I will never really comprehend. I still didn't tell anybody about the thoughts I'd been having because I was so embarrassed. Ironically though, during these years, there were also some real periods of strength and courage; I took up a kickboxing class, started running, got fit and even managed to combat my fear of flying, including flying a light aircraft and even doing a sky dive!

But after breaking up with someone who I loved dearly, knowing that his excessive drinking had also taken its toll on me - I hit rock bottom. I was signed off work as I too had become far too dependent on alcohol. I slept for up to twenty hours a day and only woke to eat, drink more vodka and go back to sleep again. The feeling of numbness was unbearable. Soon after, I found myself living back at home with my mum and following a strict routine advised by my lovely mental health counsellor: no sleeping during the day, sleep when your mum sleeps, avoid alcohol and get some exercise. It seems like obvious advice, but when you feel you have the support of somebody professional breaking things down for you and guiding you, at a time when I simply didn't have the strength to do this myself, it made this process doable for me. With small steps, my confidence grew. I started working again and even dating!

I met the most loving, attentive, caring soul and we fell in love.

When I discovered I was pregnant, I felt nothing but love and confidence that I could do this; I could actually be a Mummy because I had the most amazing partner, and we were going to be the strongest, most loving family unit a child could wish for.

Seven months pregnant, with a sparkling diamond ring on my finger I felt safe and secure, something I hadn't felt since my early teens. But then the truth began to emerge. His lies began to unravel over the following weeks. With my blood pressure sky high I was admitted to hospital and advised to try to keep calm for the baby's sake. I couldn't comprehend how this person had deceived me for so long and why. And I was terrified once again;

I couldn't be a single mum! I wasn't strong enough. I suffered with depression, anxiety and obsessive- compulsive behaviours. I wouldn't be a good mother on my own.

This isn't what I had planned.

Our daughter was born almost five weeks early, weighing 5lb 15 and not breathing, but she was whisked away and made a full recovery. Words of wisdom from my father encouraged me to accept that life wasn't going to be as I had planned, but that didn't mean it was going to destroy me, as it would have done in the past. I just needed to think differently and have a different approach. After a week in hospital my miracle baby and I were going home and I found the strength and energy to ensure that she was looked after to the very best of my ability. For the first time in my life it wasn't about me, or my depression, or anxiety issues, and as this beautiful little person continued to fight, so did I.

I fought through the obsessive thoughts about her safety and other worries such as SIDS. I knew I was being over protective, paranoid and not doing myself any favours because I needed some quality sleep in order to function. As my tiny baby grew bigger and stronger, I eventually relaxed, and I became more in control of my anxiety.

After much research, investigating and questioning on my part, it became apparent to me that my daughter's father was suffering from mental illness himself. While the anger and heartache was still very much in me, I remembered my father's advice, and just because we were not going to be the family unit I had planned for my little girl, that did not necessarily mean that she couldn't still have two parents in her life to love, protect and guide her. I realised that my idea of the 'perfect' family life wasn't necessarily the only way to raise an emotionally secure child.

I set about trying to help my daughter's father to get the help he so desperately needed.

Although he had lied to me and broken my heart, I couldn't fault him for the level of effort he applied when it came to our daughter. After a few months he was on track with regards to a diagnosis for his own mental illness, commenced counselling and obtained the right medication to help to treat him. I had mixed feelings of hate, pity and surprisingly respect towards him because he was prepared to do everything and anything in his power to make himself a good father to our daughter, which he undoubtedly loved with his heart and soul.

Our daughter knows no different to the routine set in place with assistance from mediators. She is equally in love with both her mummy and her daddy. Our little girl is an amazingly intelligent, confident and content four year old. Her father and I have a mutual respect for one another and we co-parent successfully, even managing to confide in one another from time to time about our mental illness ups and downs. Our little lady does and always will feel the emotional love and security of two parents, which I had so feared she may not.

My greatest fear was proven incorrect; just because a family break up was the trigger for my own depression and anxiety, it did not mean that my daughter would experience the same.

Since my little darling has been around, I have managed to retrain at college in Hairdressing. I have set myself up as self- employed, and I am able to work around my daughter's routine.

Although I still suffer with depression, and looking back I feel sorry for my younger self, I truly believe that I would not be the person I am today without my experiences. Counselling, CBT (cognitive behavioural therapy) and my medication has provided me with the tools and the knowledge I need to enable me to ride the waves of life. There will always be the ups and the downs for me and I accept that now. I know the warning signs and I can see when depression is creeping back into my life. I recognise it and I am aware of what I need to do in order to get myself back on track again. As a hairdresser you need to be just as good at listening as you do cutting hair, and my huge amount of experience and empathy for others enables me to relate to others on a personal level. I like to think that if my story or experiences can help or reassure anybody in any way then I'm pleased to be able to help.

As I write this, I am thirty six years old. I have no doubt that my illness will continue to play its part in my life, but it doesn't control me or scare me so much anymore. I am thankful to the NHS for providing me with some amazing support in the way of counselling (Time to Talk) and CBT, but after twenty years of chopping and changing medications, I've finally had a GP recognise that I should have had better/different support from the NHS.

I've now come to the end of the list of different anti -depressant medication that my GP's are able to prescribe, and so I have been referred to a different mental health team for better support, who have the authority to prescribe different medications which may be better suited to my specific requirements. They can also provide on-going support going forward, and so this has given me more confidence in knowing that after all these years of silently screaming, trying new medications and feeling alone, a doctor has finally given my long term illness the recognition which it requires.

Becky Digan

Life Can Change in a Moment

Anyone's circumstances can change in a moment, a moment that changes your outlook on life forever. And mine did when I was thirty seven weeks pregnant with my second child. Up until that moment, I was lucky enough to have a pretty good second pregnancy.

I remember putting our two year old boy to bed. I felt so unwell- more so than I probably ever have done. Something didn't feel right. Luckily my husband was home from work and took me to A and E, as I knew something was very unsound; like a sixth sense I suppose. I was admitted into the maternity ward and seen by different specialists to figure out why I was feeling the way I was. I was petrified.

It turned out that I had septicaemia which had led to Sepsis.

We were advised our baby had to be induced due to the dangerous situation. However, that evening my body went into spontaneous labour and he was born within three hours.

Thank God he was absolutely fine.

But I felt so ill and exhausted; you really have to dig deep in those circumstances, and looking back I don't know how I found the strength to give birth; survival mode I guess.

When he was born, for about a minute I had this intense feeling of accomplishment, and it was like the world stood still; a bubble appeared around me and it felt safe to have his warm body on my chest, to see he looked ok, and that what was happening to me hadn't affected him.

Then of course that bubble burst.

At this point I was mentally and physically broken. I just wanted to feel well enough to look after my baby and go home to be with the rest of my family, but that was not to be. My husband was allowed to sleep in the room to look after our new born at this point, which was hard for me. It made me feel pretty useless.

I was then transferred to Brighton hospital for more invasive tests and treatment. I arrived via ambulance. By this time my husband had taken our baby home. The paramedics had brought a balloon I'd been given that read "congratulations baby boy". But I felt like a failure. My baby was home and I was going further away to a hospital I didn't know. I was put in my own room and boy did I feel very low and alone. The nurses were a great support, but I almost felt like a child again; I was scared of the dark and kept asking for the door to be left open just so that I could hear voices.

After two weeks in hospital, with persuasion, the doctors agreed to let me have the IV antibiotics at home. They were to be administered by a nurse, daily, for a further two weeks. As I was getting ready to go home, one of the nurses came in and said to me, "You're one lucky lady." I know now how lucky I was to have survived Sepsis, but at the time I didn't feel lucky at all. I was devastated to have missed that first two weeks at home with my new baby and I'd missed my eldest son incredibly.

The journey home was odd. I'd expected to feel elated at the prospect of going home but I didn't. I didn't understand why I wasn't feeling happy. I thankfully have never suffered any kind of depression in my life, but looking back I think I was heading down that path. All I could see for a long time was a grey, bleak world. I felt I was in a very dark, black hole and couldn't see a way out and didn't know how to express this. I suppose I was desperate for someone to understand me, but no one could hear what I was really trying to say. And in fact I don't think I really understood how I was feeling anyway, so I just went about daily life not telling anyone about this darkness. After all, I had no reason to feel this way- I had just survived Sepsis and given birth to a beautiful baby boy to complete our perfect little family.

As the days passed by I watched my husband remain strong; he had been so calm throughout all of this, and I realised how lucky I was to have him, not only as a husband but as a best friend and a father to our children too. My incredibly amazing mum was there every morning to help when my husband had to go back to work. She was and always has been a driving force behind my ability to never give up.

But despite trying to find the positives and attempting to remain grateful, I still didn't feel like myself. During a routine check –up I remember a midwife asking me "But how are YOU coping now?" I just broke down. Someone had seen through the exterior and I felt a sense of relief. I finally felt free to open up and spoke about how I was struggling mentally. I believe talking about it most definitely helped me to heal.

For a period of time I developed OCD. I was hyper aware of germs and didn't want to ever experience what I just had again. I started to become obsessed with cleaning, keeping everything sterile and using antibacterial agents on everything, probably to a detrimental effect. I am now much less concerned with that and know that I can't protect myself or my children from everything; some things are beyond my control and I accept that. I do still worry from time to time, but I don't let it control my life and dominate my thoughts.

I now view life with a different perspective; I'm grateful for what I have and have witnessed strength in people that has empowered me to emulate the same. Sometimes we go through terrible times, but some of us are lucky enough to come through. My mantra is to focus on the present rather than the past. I've learnt to live for the moment, because a moment is all it takes to change our lives forever.

Sarah Marsh

The Better Way to Life
from the perspective of the rescue cat

As I stretch out from my Sunday afternoon nap, I feel safe and secure. I feel warm and cozy in the heat of the sun as it streams through the patio window, and I lazily watch the autumn leaves falling and dancing around, riding on the breeze. My mind flits and my thoughts quickly turn to consider my dinner. I paw my way across the house to my water bowl and pause to lap up some fresh water. As I quench my thirst, I shift my attention to the present moment and consider how truly fortunate I am.

It is easy to forget sometimes; how fortunate I am. I often find myself full of dread, consumed by bad thoughts, so I try and remind myself every day what a great life I am living and focus on every little thing that does bring me joy and happiness in the moment, which are often the simplest things....

I am very self sufficient; I can achieve anything that I want to. I can jump over the wall. I can come and go as I please. I can look after myself (most of the time) so I do not appreciate being molly-coddled. My independence is important to me and I want to maintain it, but don't let that fool you; I don't always want to be strong on my own. At times I do feel weak and vulnerable, and in those instances, I do appreciate your help and support.

They say with the right amount of stress, one can outperform themselves. I know and have proved that to be true; I am more than capable of jumping over the highest of fences if I must or want. However, under too much pressure I can make mistakes and bad choices. If I start to feel out of control, I might recoil, protest and bite at my perceived threat. In those circumstances it is usually a good idea to give me the space I need. But do not abandon me. I just need a moment.

When I want to, I love having the run of the house, and being queen of my casa; being able to do as I please and be what I want to be and where I want to be. And oh, how I love cuddles; one can never have too much of that. People often underestimate what a cuddle can do. There is a lot to be said about a bit of real connection; a physical touch here and there can be most consoling.

A bit of human touch is particularly reassuring, especially when I am feeling down (sometimes for no particular reason at all, whilst other times there are plenty of legitimate reasons). A really good squeeze, a hug, a full-on embrace, whichever way, it makes all the difference to feeling understood, reassured and supported. Never underestimate this unspoken gesture, no matter how small or insignificant it might seem. Such action often speaks much louder than (sometimes unnecessary) words to bring a considerable amount of comfort. I don't get why humans prefer their phones to stroking me- step forward and give me a hug, and maybe a nose-bump too!

I do also love conversations, especially the ones that are two-way; no one enjoys a monologue, not really, even if they say they do. We all want to be part of the conversation and to have our side of the story heard. I do this by meowing first, making slightly different noises to ensure my mama, papa and adopted sister know that I am not pleased by the late lie-in, or being ignored and overlooked for the iPhone. When I need attention, I make sure someone knows about it! I need some acknowledgement, a stroke, a kiss. And sometimes I just need food! I know what I want, and I am not afraid to ask for it. But when I am quiet, leave me be. I am hiding in my own thoughts and I need it that way, just for a little while.

During these times, I do not like to be talked at or be told to do things that I do not want to; I am not ready, and I prefer to do it on my own terms at a time of my choosing. So, do not patronise me, do not talk to me like I am a child, and do not offer unwanted words, doing so causes more frustration and upset. Take a step back and if needed, talk soothingly. Redirect my focus onto the positives, or simply provide signs that show me that I am being heard despite my stillness and quietness. That to me, at that point in time, is much more helpful and valuable.

However secure we are in ourselves, it is always heartening to hear something pleasant about oneself. I love to know that I am a "good girl" and need reassurance that I am wanted, needed and loved, because sometimes I think so badly of myself I just need reminding that actually I am better than I dare to imagine myself to be. Mostly, I just need to know that I can come to you if and when I am ready.

I love to sleep, but perhaps I do not really get enough, and conceivably this is something that I could always do with more of. Sleep deprivation is more harmful than anything else - after all this is one of the leading interrogation techniques that the authority employs! Falling asleep is particularly problematic when one is filled with angst and frustration from the day. If my human parents have gone on holiday, I often think the worst *perhaps they have left me – are they coming back? Will there be food again?* And what can one really do when flooded with such thoughts whilst in bed, late at night? Logically I know that I should just acknowledge the thought and park it for the next day, so that I can be productive, energised from a good night's sleep. So, I have learnt to snuggle up, feel the warmth and comfort of the bed, and breathe slowly and steadily, shifting my mind to the few things that bring me peace, calm, and happiness. Slowly and surely, I drift off to the land of nod ... Zzzz...

I love food and I know that I have plenty, though I admit, my eyes are always bigger than my stomach, and often I want more than what I really need. Is that because I am greedy and want more than my fair share? Or is it because I never used to have enough, so now I over compensate? Or do I use food as a source of comfort? Regardless, one thing is for sure; I will never go hungry or thirsty, and that is something that I should always be thankful for.

The simple pleasure of having food in the mouth and stomach is indescribable. Food is not simply used to satisfy my hunger, but is one of life's greatest pleasures, and I do need to remind myself how lucky I am. Dinner time with my family is such a sensory experience when I pay close attention to the moment and stay fully present; the sound of the clanging plates informs me of the prospect of dinner time, the sight of the food brings anticipation, the aroma of food reinforces that expectation, and the taste of the food hitting my palate affirms the yummy deliciousness that is being devoured.

Thinking back, I have lived here for over ten years now, and you would not guess that I was a rescued cat looking at me now with my shiny coat, filled-out bod, and non-stop purring. It would be difficult for you to imagine how I had looked and felt when I first arrived - I was scrawny, stick thin, stressed and pulling my fur out. The cat home did their best to care for me, but my owners taking me home with them is the greatest thing that has ever happened to me.

Yes, I have been through a lot, so occasionally I do feel insecure and anxious, as I cannot help but be reminded and relive the trauma that I suffered. My thoughts do sometimes drift back to a time when I was not as comfortable and content as I am now. But whilst it is not pleasant to think of the ancient past, it is nevertheless useful to be reminded of where I could have been versus where I am now, providing that I do not continue to ruminate, and instead refocus and be present. I try to always remind myself that after all, nothing is quite as good as feeling and knowing that I am home, that I am fed, that I am loved, and actually the past has been overcome and led me to where I want and need to be.

CQ

"When I find myself being critical of my body,

I try to remember all of the reasons that I owe it gratitude."

Moses

The knot in my stomach tightened; I couldn't believe this was happening again. The fluid on the back of your neck was reading too high, your heart beat a little slow. There was a one in three chance you had Down's Syndrome. Further tests revealed you didn't in fact have a chromosomal disorder of any kind. You did however, have a hole in your heart, which at first they deemed operable after birth, but as the pregnancy progressed it became apparent that your heart condition was far worse; your tiny body was struggling, fluid was gathering around all your vital organs. The doctors urged me to end your life. They were concerned that I might start to replicate the same symptoms, and that all evidence suggested you wouldn't make it to term anyway.

I refused their pleas. I had to give you a chance, however small that was. I'd heard your heartbeat, seen your little hands wave when they'd scanned me. I'd felt you move inside me. My heart beat for yours. I had to hold on for you, as any mother would; your life was not over.

I remember the day they scanned me for the last time. In all honesty, I knew you'd gone. I'd felt your life extinguish the day before; a dullness had swept over me. It was the night the wolves came, guarding and then pacing my bed. It didn't make it any easier as the sonographer placed the transducer on my belly that day. I looked at the screen willing for your heart to beat. And then there they were; those three soul destroying words, "I'm so sorry…"

It's disbelief that hits you at first; the refusal to accept the situation. Your hopes are still pinned to a second opinion. I wanted to scream at the sonographer, the nurses and the consultant. I felt the sting of tears behind my eyes and when they fell, I thought they'd never stop. I crumbled. I heaved. I made noises like some wild animal howling into the night, knowing that I'd have to give birth to your lifeless body and hand you over.

I carried you inside me for a further two days before that happened. It's a day I will never forget. I was so frightened. I didn't know what you would look like;

they'd warned me you might be a little red as you had passed a few days before. I was worried I would break you if I pushed too hard; you were still so small and fragile.

The nurses left us alone to deliver you. The labour was short and relatively painless. When I pushed you out I couldn't bear to look at you. We called for a nurse who whisked you away and cleaned you up. We sat in silence. I don't ever recall feeling so numb. I was empty.

And then there it was. The gentle knock at the door. You were ready, if we wanted to see you. They brought you in in a basket, wrapped in blankets and a hat, so we called you Moses.

And you were perfect.

You were not much bigger than the palm of my hand, but you had ten very tiny fingers and toes. Nails. Ears. Eyes. You had everything that any little boy would have. A flood of conflicting emotions washed over me; love for you, anger that this had happened, fear that this empty void would never be filled, bitterness that I would never get to bring you home. We spent the afternoon with you until it was time to hand you back, knowing that next time I'd see you, you'd be in a box.

I left the hospital a changed woman. The ensuing days were a blur of sleepless nights and long days. Looking back now, the determination to love and appreciate your three siblings was the only thing that got me through. I felt selfish to cry tears for you when I had the chance to sit and play with the children I already had.

I remember everything seeming very mechanical after a while; I was running on empty and my emotions fell flat- I had no energy to cry, laugh, love or hate. Day- to -day chores got completed and the house and the children were running like a well- oiled machine, but it was all very robotic and unnatural. When the day of your cremation arrived, I felt sick. And alone. Looking back, perhaps I was a little selfish in thinking that I had been the only one affected by this. At the time, I'd been the only one to feel you, to know your movements, to talk to you, to embrace you. Nobody else had really known you. I wondered why anyone else would even care. But there were others who had invested their time, thoughts and love into you, with the hope of one day holding you too, but it was hard to see that at the time.

I think perhaps I even felt angry at your Dad; that he would even dare to compare his loss to mine. I'm not saying that's right, but it was how I felt at the time. I was so consumed by my own pain that I couldn't recognise the pain your loss had caused others.

I won't lie- losing you put a strain on our marriage. Instead of turning to each other and holding one another up, we fell apart, each of us turning inwards with our grief. I don't recall ever once talking with your Dad about how either he or I felt about losing you. We carried on as if nothing happened, never really acknowledging the huge impact that your loss had on either of us. And that led to a lot of misunderstanding and miscommunication. We started to live very separate lives and those unspoken wounds began to fester.

It is six years since you left this earth and your Dad and I did eventually find our way back to each other. You've gained another sister in that time; a joyous, spirited Being full of light and laughter just like the others. Your four siblings talk about you- they ask questions and place flowers at your grave.

I feel at peace when I think of you now. It took a long time. Losing you taught me to accept that some things are beyond our control, death being the ultimate example of such. Acceptance also helped me to heal and move forward because denial and refusing to accept circumstances only traps us in the past, chaining us to a time 'before' that no longer exists.

Adjusting is incremental and cannot be rushed. But we did adjust. And we moved forward all the better for knowing you.

Maria Alfieri

In the Wake of the Walking Wounded

"Blessed are those who mourn, for they shall be comforted" Matthew 5:4

But this is not always the case for the ones suicide leaves behind. Among the many feelings of sadness, anger, guilt and denial that can accompany the loss of a friend or loved one, those who have lost theirs to suicide often have to contend with an extra layer of shame and stigma, as opposed to receiving the support one would in the case of another type of bereavement.

Sometimes instead of comfort, you find ignorance, judgement and fear. In place of the usual platitudes and consolation, you find either explicit or unspoken discomfort at the revelation of death by suicide, sometimes followed by implied judgement. This can come in the form of the look in people's eyes when you tell them, witnessing their sharp intake of breath, or the mixture of horror and fear sometimes inadvertently displayed. Even those whom you consider close friends can avoid speaking on the subject directly, for fear of saying the 'wrong' thing. In extreme cases you can end up experiencing pity replaced with persecution. Some people still pass very harsh judgement of the act, the individual who has died by suicide and often onto those around them. The families can experience guilt and shame 'by association'.

Even if the words are not spoken directly to you in your state of grief and mourning, how often have you heard others on the periphery of a suicide situation talk amongst themselves about it 'behind the scenes'? Maybe in the past you've even been a participant in such a discussion. People often carelessly say things like:

"How could they not see any signs?"

"Why couldn't they have talked to their family?"

"They had so much to live for!"

"But there are so many people worse off in the world!"

I have viewed instances where people with no direct relation to the individual have been angered; many still see suicide as 'selfish' and that the person has 'taken' something of value by ending their life, which so many people in worse situations would give everything for.   Even the terminology is problematic. It's often still reported people have 'committed suicide'. Such an expression attributes guilt, and up until recently in this country it was a crime.   In many countries it still is considered as such today.   Historically there have been posthumous punishments, such as denial of usual burial rights because of religious scripting around suicide being an offense against God.

All of this vilification and lack of understanding comes at a cost.   This shame and stigma does little to provide comfort for those experiencing this unique type of grief and trauma. And what does it say to the survivors of suicide attempts, for those people struggling and contemplating suicide? I am by no means an expert or a trained mental health practitioner, but I have personally lost a family member, a friend, and watched on as a dear friend lost a close family member–all to suicide within the last five years. In itself this type of loss is a traumatic event.   It has caused me to do a great deal of questioning, soul searching and research with mental health and suicide charities.

I have witnessed suicide come after a long struggle and a period of associated mental illness; so sad and shocking, but not entirely unexpected. I have also seen death by suicide come as a bolt from the blue, accompanied by no build up, or even hints or signs that a person was struggling mentally and emotionally. In fact, it has come so completely from the left field, I've known confused relatives to question the cause of death and go into deep denial.

When you don't meet the standard criteria for grief and mourning, you can be left feeling detached and isolated. How can anyone else understand what you yourself are desperately struggling to make sense of?   How can you tell people how they died when you fear they will be judged and stigmatised in the way you have observed friends, colleagues and family members openly condemn suicide and it's victims in the past?

You can feel angry at the person themselves; how could they not see that they haven't ended any pain but merely passed it on to those left behind in their wake? You can feel guilt that you weren't able to prevent it from happening and that this person was evidently in terrible pain and could not reach out to you. As well as the initial shock you can find yourself searching through memories for clues and closure that will likely never come. You may initially struggle with how and what to tell people, and even well-meaning friends and family will rarely know what to say in response. It's uncomfortable at best, as it is so little talked about.

In 2017 there were just over six thousand instances of death by suicide in the UK alone. The number of family, friends, colleagues and other acquaintances whose lives have been touched in that single year by these deaths must run into the hundreds of thousands-so why is there still such a taboo around the subject? If this is a reality for so many people, why is it still so little talked about in the open?

One factor is the current social rhetoric around mental illness and 'negative' emotions. We need to give ourselves and others permission to feel and speak our authentic emotional reality before we can address problems with it. We need to look at why we are so desperate just to 'fix' negative emotions that we are not comfortable with, and learn the value of sitting with those emotions, and the art of talking and listening as a means of validation. Such a simple thing as feeling like you can speak your feelings without being 'wrong' or 'shamed' can make such a difference to your ability to cope with them. The opposite can be highly damaging.

I remember going to the GP suffering from what I now recognise as post natal depression, and all my doctor could do was to point out that I really didn't have anything to be depressed about. He spoke at length about people in third world countries and how primitive societies were happier in general and had a great appreciation for the small things we take for granted. The doctor's response only fuelled shame and guilt, and fostered a reluctance to talk any further about it. That could have been extremely damaging had I not had others who were less dismissive.

My midwife was fantastic and easily addressed my upset with a simple, "I'm sorry you feel like that, it's likely a mixture of hormones and exhaustion and a lot of people get it…" Just having someone recognise that this was a result of physical changes in my body, a huge alteration to my life in the form of a brand new human I was responsible for, and that I wasn't the only person to feel like this instead of making me feel ungrateful and ashamed, was enough to set me on the path to recovery from that instance.

Another thing we tend to do as a society which minimises mental health issues is through our storytelling where we often glorify 'silent' struggles. We perpetuate romanticised ideals of strong, silent warriors; this is particularly prevalent for men, embedded deeply in society's toxic masculine scripting. It is likely a contributing factor as to why three times as many men die by suicide, whereas statistically speaking more women are recorded as having considered it.

Men are often expected to internalise and be strong for their family and in times of crisis can receive little support themselves. Our definition of strength seems to be synonymous with controlling our emotional state and being able to stay on top of everything, all alone. We don't see speaking out and authenticity as strength; in fact sometimes it's painted as a weakness or 'attention seeking'- as if seeking attention from and connection with others is something abhorrent, rather than a natural human need. We seem to forget we are social animals, and connection and compassion are the keystones to what makes us thrive as a species.

We are denying our innate nature to fit a socially constructed script of what's ideal and acceptable. Separation is positioned as strength. Kindness is posited as weakness. One phrase I see bandied about a lot these days on social media in particular is "be kind to others as you never know what they are going through". While it does have its merits in spreading the seemingly obvious message that you can't diagnose someone's situation and mental/physical health from the way they appear outwardly, this is one of my least favourite inspirational phrases of the moment. Why not just 'be kind?' Why can't we extend compassion, empathy and kindness without the caveat that the value we carry is in how much we can strive and thrive alone. Not to mention there's a reason we often don't know what other people are going through, as we have made it uncomfortable to OPENLY struggle. We label, we judge and we repress for fear of being associated with negativity and 'neediness' because of how society perceives these things.

A topic currently provoking a lot of discussion among suicide charities and support groups is how we would benefit from changing the way we speak and therefore think about mental health and suicide. We must learn to see and speak about those whose lives have been ended by suicide as what they are; victims. They are victims of a varying number of things to varying degrees- sometimes circumstance, long standing illness, pressure of societal expectations or repeated unbidden intrusive thoughts. The only sure thing about suicide is that it is absolutely never someone's easy option. It is not something that means someone has been weak or 'given up'. One cannot control their recovery from mental illness or sudden intrusive suicidal thoughts anymore than they can manipulate their recovery from cancer or anticipate themselves having a heart attack.

It is useful to consider suicidal thoughts and tendencies as a variant of other 'physical' illnesses-being suicidal can be anywhere on a sliding spectrum. It doesn't even always mean someone wants to die. It can present in the form of constant unwanted impulses and thoughts which are never/will never be acted upon. It can come in the form of simply wanting the overwhelming feelings of depression or stress to stop, and it can even come as a desire to do something to simply feel the will to LIVE once again.

And lastly be we mustn't be afraid to be more honest, with ourselves and each other. I'd be inauthentic if I spent this whole piece speaking about lifting shame and stigma surrounding mental health and suicide and omitted to talk about my own struggles with depression and anxiety. More importantly if I omitted that I have experienced suicidal thoughts myself. I would never have framed them as such prior to my experiences over the last five years, but in retrospect that is what they were.

In isolation from various instances of depression and from a lifelong tussle with varying degrees of anxiety, I have experienced thoughts in the form of a 'flash' of calm inspiration, and urges in the midst of overwhelm and anxiety as a desperate wish that the feeling would just end. I think it's important to say that on neither of those occasions did I actually experience wanting to die. For instance, on the first occasion it was simply a fleeting intrusive thought with no impulse or desire accompanying it. I was just standing looking out of a top floor window while waiting for a lift in a hospital, while my son was quite seriously ill but recovering, and I thought to myself out of nowhere- "If I were to lose him, that would be the window I would jump from." As quick as a flash it was gone again, and I knew there is no way I would actually have acted upon it. I can't even begin to imagine what it would be like living constantly bombarded by thoughts like this, which can come entirely without the urge to act upon them at all, as I have come to learn some people do.

I've learned a lot and become more open in the last few years, and as a result people feel they can be more open with me. I've had friends tell me they've been so overwhelmed with work and life that they've considered driving their car into a wall-not so that they would die necessarily, but just so would they'd be hospitalised long enough to rest if they survived.

I've had a friend experience such excruciating physical pain from an accident that she swears if someone had told her at the time of the accident that her pain would be prolonged, without relief, and that she'd have to overcome it herself (in the way we often do with people with mental anguish) she would have begged them to end her life right then and there. By being open, we open the way for others to do the same. By seeking to understand rather than judge, we gain the power to help prevent. By giving comfort instead of condemnation we set people free to feel and heal.

Treat each other gently people, not just to protect those walking wounded battling physical and emotional pain we can't see, but because quite simply we are all equally deserving of kindness and compassion-and because it's a good way to live!

Cheryle Brown

Parenting and Mental Health

Everybody knows that being a parent is stressful in even the most ordinary of circumstances. When your child has additional needs or serious or lifelong illnesses, that stress is multiplied. Elsewhere in this book you will read about my mental health difficulties following diagnosis and treatment for breast cancer, but my story began many years earlier when we were unable to conceive.

Growing up I looked to my future as being married with children; this was further cemented when I was about fifteen years old and our next-door neighbour had a baby. The feeling of love from holding this tiny little boy was just overwhelming. From that moment I knew I had to be a mum. Throughout my education I had always aimed for success and had a strong belief that I could do anything I wanted if I worked hard enough. There was no space in my mind for 'circumstances beyond my control', because I believed I was in control of every aspect of my life and felt responsible for anything that went wrong. That included my inability to conceive.

As far as I was concerned, it was my body, therefore it was my fault. When the IVF was unsuccessful, I felt even more to blame. All I wanted was to have a baby. Each month, each period, each failed cycle of IVF shattered my dream over and over, bringing more self-blame and hopelessness, building month on month.

All I could see was everyone one else having what I couldn't. Everywhere there were reminders about how I'd failed at being a woman and failed at the only thing I wanted out of life. Everyday brought fresh tears; at home, at work, at the shops, everywhere until I couldn't do it anymore. I could no longer force a smile and pretend I was OK.

Being diagnosed with depression just gave me another reason to blame myself; this time for not being able to control my emotions, for not being able to make myself feel better. I felt ashamed and completely at fault. I didn't want to admit that I had depression and I didn't want to take anti-depressants. I thought if I just tried a bit harder, I could make myself well again.

It took time, anti-depressants and cognitive behavioural therapy to get over this episode of depression. I learned to accept that we would never conceive our own child and instead turned my attention to adoption.

I will always remember the day we met our children, our first day out together, and the day we brought them home. Suddenly, there were two little ones asleep upstairs and we were finally parents. It was the best but most surreal moment. As with most new parents adjusting to the care needs of a child is challenging, but for us it wasn't a new-born but two pre-school aged children. Two children who had had the worst start in life imaginable, had been moved from carer to carer, and were hoping we would be their forever family. Two children who had experienced being let down and learned that adults were unreliable. Two children who hadn't received consistent parenting and knew more than most how to push boundaries.

Two children who would now receive the best care we could possibly give them. I had always imagined being a stay at home mum, even before infertility and adoption, and after years of waiting I wasn't going to miss a single moment. It wasn't easy; I didn't have a ready-made network from antenatal class, all my friends were at work, my husband was at work, all other family many miles away.

This sense of isolation was not something I had expected, but after all we'd been through to get to this point, I couldn't complain. My new life as a mum was so far away from my dreams, and so far away from the experience of other families. Everything I said was met with "but they all do that", "it's just a stage", and other platitudes. Even the social workers minimised the behaviours we were living with, the extent of their support was to offer parenting strategies.

It became easier to pretend that everything was alright to the outside world, with only my husband and I knowing the reality. We had fought so hard to become parents and it wasn't the happy ideal we'd hoped for, but how do you tell people this? How do you explain that you can't cope? That the one thing you wanted out of life is now the one thing that's making life so difficult? That you have no choice but to keep going because if you give up on the children, what then? How do you make people take your concerns seriously? How do you make the school understand and change their approach? How do you not feel like a bad parent when you cry yourself to sleep and wish things were different?

All the neglect and trauma they had experienced in their early life was being thrown back at us everyday through their behaviour and we just wanted it to stop. You want to make it better, to soak up their pain. You want to be more than a sticking plaster on their emotions, you want to be the magic wand. And when you can't do this you feel helpless. You feel like you are failing the children just like everyone else has failed them before.

And you blame yourself for not being able to make it better.

Years down the line and our children are approaching adulthood with their own aspirations and thoughts for the future. The neglect they experienced in their birth family has had a profound and long-lasting impact on their development and may very well continue to cause them difficulties in the future. I know that in providing a safe, loving environment for them to grow up in we have given them a chance at a future that would otherwise have been out of reach, but it hasn't been easy and certainly wasn't the parenting journey I had imagined. The truth is there is no such thing as 'the perfect family' and we need to be talking more openly about parenting struggles and providing a better network of support for parents and carers of children.

Karen Horsley

Kate and Her Wolves

Hello dark wolf,

Shadow self.

I know many know you by another name.

Some call you depression.

I know you have more than one name and I am unafraid to take mine back.

You run in my veins, but you are not a part of me.

You are a sinister resident in these woods.

Temporary,

Moving,

Shifting,

Dancing.

You are not who I am; you are the shadows made from light.

This duality is your fear,

But I promise you that you are safe here.

I honour you, humble visitor.

I offer you warmth, fire, nourishment, love.

You are just one of my wolf pack, but I am the leader.

Kate Morgan

"Looking back now, my suicide attempt was never really about wanting to end my life, but about wanting to end my pain and seeing no other way in which to do that. I am so thankful that I didn't succeed. I have absolutely everything to live for. I just couldn't see it back then."

Sometimes, you can't see the wood for the trees.

Living on the surface

We live on the surface too afraid to go within and explore the depths of our own cave. We talk about stepping out of the cave and into the light, out of the shadows and into the sun, and yet the vast expanse of our internal territory lies dormant, un-awakened, unexplored.

When the life force of the landscape within is little understood, change is fear inducing; our internal environment fights for homeostasis. Eruptions, peaks and valleys cannot be navigated. We run from our discomfort, terrified by the tsunami of our emotions.

Dive beneath the surface of you. Swim through your oceans. Excavate your lands. Climb your mountains. For in understanding ourselves, we find safety. Those strong internal foundations keep us steady when the outside world begins to shake.

Imagine

Heavy clouds cover the sky

Darkness falls

I close my eyes

Lift my face towards the clouds

Feel the breeze

As rain falls down

Grey clouds, grey skies

A damp grey mist

My eyes still closed

I dream, I wish

Imagine white clouds

With sun breaking through

And picture a rainbow

In my sky so blue

Karen Horsley

Step into the Sunshine

Step out from the shadows

Deny those cloudy days

Greet the warmth of sunshine

The glow of golden rays

With dark times behind

The memories remain

Moving forward we will find

Distance from the pain

Past hurt can be forgotten when blinded by the sun

Its glare provides a shield

Of luminous protection

Our sunshine is the future

The hope that keeps us strong

For if we live within our dreams

The sun will linger on

Karen Horsley

Final Message

Owning our story can be hard, but not nearly as difficult as spending our lives running from it. Embracing our vulnerabilities is risky but not nearly as dangerous as giving up on love and belonging and joy-the experiences that make us vulnerable. Only when we are brave enough to explore the darkness will we discover the infinite power of our light.

-Brené Brown, *The Gifts of Imperfection*

Some things are hard to say out loud, but everyone has a story to tell. In finally finding my voice and the courage to read aloud my own unread chapters, my feelings of shame and unworthiness began to lift. I realised very quickly that *it's not just me*. In collating *The Silent Scream* anthology I found healing through a shared vulnerability with a group of strangers that liberated me from my loneliness and unworthiness. In facing my fears I found connection without rules, outside the lines and in places where I thought I wouldn't. And some of us shared nothing more in common that the experience of struggle and despair, and a willingness to expose our darkness, so that others might find the infinite power of light. Like one candle lighting another, our stories spread hope. It doesn't mean that we will never struggle again. But in accepting our own darkness, we can be present with others in theirs- compassion becomes real when we recognise our shared humanity. So next time you find yourself struggling, ashamed, feeling unworthy and screaming silently inside, remember that we are all human. We are all messy and imperfect. Vulnerability is not weakness. Reach out. Connection is critical because we all have the basic need to feel accepted and to believe that we belong and are valued for who we are.[v]

Together, let's navigate the pages of our lives to become the authors of new chapters yet to be written.

Endnotes

i   www.bbc.co.uk September 2018

ii   www.mind.org.uk June 2018

iii   www.samaritans.org.uk September 2018 Suicide Statistics Report

iv   The Power of Now: A Guide to Spiritual Enlightenment, Eckhart Tolle, Namaste Publishing, 1997

v   www.BreneBrown.com Downloads and Guides - September 2019

Resources

Addiction:

Alcoholics Anonymous UK – www.alcoholics-anonymous.org.uk

Gamblers Anonymous UK – www.gamblersanonymous.org.uk

Narcotics Anonymous UK – ukna.org

Overeaters Anonymous – oa.org

Eating Disorders:

Beat Eating Disorders – www.beateatingdisorders.org.uk

Mental Health:

Mind – www.mind.org.uk

Preedy Psychology – www.preedypsychology.co.uk
Dr Katherine Preedy is a Clinical Psychologist working in private practice in Reigate, Surrey. She works with people with all kinds of issues including anxiety and depression and has a special interest in supporting people with trauma, PTSD, birth trauma and Post-natal issues.

Samaritans – www.samaritans.org

The Good Limbo – thegoodlimbo.com
The Good Limbo is a mental health community run by those with mental health issues for those with mental health issues. They have forums, a live chat, arcades, blog posts and podcasts. Everybody is welcome!

Time to Change – www.time-to-change.org.uk

Sexual Abuse:

Truth Project – Independent Inquiry into Child Sexual Abuse
www.truthproject.org.uk

NAPAC – The National Association for People Abused in Childhood
napac.org.uk

Photography Credits

A
Alfieri, Maria 68
Aptem 160
Austin, Rikki 244

B
Banks, Clay 142
Bender, Max 133
Blucker, Jake 70
Blum, Brina 117

C
Campbell, Christopher 94
Castro, Jessica 12
Catalog, Thought 204
Christopher, Taelynn 196

D
D, Jules 124
Deets, Charlie 174
Dinc, Altinay 266
du Preez, Priscilla 121

E
Ensey, Chris 112

G
Glenn, Kyle 232

H
Hardy, Matt 108

I
Ian, The 150
Inglez, Manuel 34

J
Jasmin, Joel 268
Jensen, Mathias 214

K
Klauer, Florian 10
Komori, Masaaki 222

L
Lawton, Chris 194
Lazarenko, Serafima 262
Le Dinh, Hoach 156
Li, Yeon 54
Lopez, Alex 122

M
Maloney, Doug 81
Marino, Joy 276
Marisescu, Vlad 128
Matzinger, Simon 249
Mello, Aaron 270
Muller, Valentin 272

N
Nohassi, Mohamed 24
Noonan, Nikolas 84

P
Parekh, Kunj 243

Q
Quintero, Camila 180

R
Rounce, Shane 7

S
Schnabel, Christoph 26
Sepehr 138
Shuliahin, Nik 176
Soe Min, Aung 255
Srikanta 20
Street, Jamie 216
Subia, Jared 88
Swancar, Adrian 38

T
Tagalog, Brian Patrick 274
Tinneberg, Jan 224
Tran, Anthony 200
Tudorache, Alexandru 82

W
Westbrook, Flora vi, 9, 17, 18, 30, 33, 44, 45, 49, 58, 60, 65, 76, 90, 96, 98, 100, 103, 106, 148, 149, 152, 168, 208, 213, 250

Contributors

Maria Alfieri - www.mariaalfieri.com
Maria is an English teacher and mother of four. She spent eighteen months out in communities world-wide - reaching out to people, empowering them to find their voices, and help tell their stories in the hope of shedding light on the importance of stepping away from shame and speaking up. The resulting book provides 70+ stories, poems, and quotations from over 40 contributors.

I'd like to acknowledge all the contributors and thank you for your courage in coming forward with your own silent scream. As collaborators we make our mess our message: **we are not alone.**

Cheryle Brown - theyearofnofear2019.com
Cheryle writes a blog at Bonheur Health and Happiness, which is dedicated to finding a healthier, happier and more conscious way of living. Follow her on her *Year of No Fear* journey, sparked by her written contributions for *The Silent Scream* anthology.

Michelle Catanach - michellecatanach.co.uk
Writer, Artist, Illustrator and mental health advocate – Michelle believes that authentic self-expression is a birth right and that we (adults) have a responsibility to heal in order to allow our children to grow. She is the compiler of Amazon #1 bestselling anthologies *Uncaged: The Rise of the Badass* and *Boys Do Cry* and is also the founder of Inside Out Publishing, a self-publishing platform for parents, teachers and entrepreneurs to create children's wellness books. Michelle runs writing retreats, workshops and programmes for adults and children to tap into their innate creativity, and write books that shift paradigms and transform worlds. Her clients have become bestselling authors, engaging speakers and continue to positively impact the world with their message.

Katie Finch - www.Kitkatyoga.wixsite.com/kitkatyoga
Katie is a yoga teacher and therapist specialising in supporting people who experience anxiety and depression. She uses a combination of yoga practices like meditation, breathwork and mindfulness combined with talking therapies to help people uncover how to find their true happiness.

Tuesday Guidera - www.kidsthatyoga.com
Tuesday provides yoga classes for kids in a fun and creative way.

Karen Horsley - blueskydays365.com
Karen is the author of two collections of poetry. *I am the Stars in the Sky*, which follows her emotional journey through cancer and mental illness - themed by fear, despair, isolation, change, and peace, and culminating with a message of hope. *Kaleidoscopic Beauty* explores love, loss and the beauty of the natural world. Both are available to purchase online. Her poetry has also featured in *Voice of Eve, Beneath the Rainbow*, and in the anthology *Further Within Darkness and Light*.

Emily Jacob - reconnected.life
Emily is a coach, NLP master practitioner and changemaker. She set up ReConnected life to help rape survivors shed the shame and blame and live a reconnected life. Emily's book, *To Report or Not to Report: Survivor Testimony of the (In)Justice System* is available to buy online. Emily is also a featured author in *Uncaged: The Rise of the Woman Badass* and *Kintsugi*.

Kate Morgan - www.twowolveshealing.com
Kate has a PhD in mental health and is a qualified Angelic Reiki practitioner. She works with individuals to help them on their journey of recovery from trauma, depression, anxiety and emotional distress to reach a place of healing, harmony and acceptance where they can understand their authentic self and their life purpose.

Ashley Peterson - mentalhealthathome.org
Ashley is a mental health nurse who speaks openly about her own ongoing battle with a major depressive disorder. Her blog *Mental Health at Home* aims to raise awareness about mental illness and create a community where people can feel comfortable speaking openly about mental health. Ashley is also author of *Psych Meds Made Simple: How & Why They Do What They Do* available for purchase online.

Gurpreet Raulia
Gurpreet's debut poetry collection *Looking for Summer* is available to purchase online.

Flora Westbrook - www.flotography.co.uk
Flo is passionate about capturing raw emotions and the stories of those she photographs. She uses photography as a tool for healing and runs "love yourself" photo sessions.

Lightning Source UK Ltd.
Milton Keynes UK
UKHW050858090220
358284UK00002BA/21